AF572452

NATIONAL DRAWING INVITATIONAL

THE ARKANSAS ARTS CENTER

NATIONAL DRAWING INVITATIONAL

February 2 - April 21, 1996

Townsend Wolfe

Sponsored by
Williams & Anderson
Kathleen and James Atkins
Annette and Phil Herrington
Marilynn and Dr. Robert A. Porter, Jr.

THE ARKANSAS ARTS CENTER

6th Biennial National Drawing Invitational

The Arkansas Arts Center
MacArthur Park, 9th & Commerce Streets
Little Rock, Arkansas 72202
P.O. Box 2137, 72203

Director and Chief Curator: Townsend Wolfe
Curator of Art: Ruth Pasquine
Registrar: Thom Hall
Curatorial Assistant: Lynnette Watts
Assistant Registrar: Hal Prestwood

Printed in U.S.A.
by International Graphics Inc.
Little Rock, Arkansas

ISBN 1-884240-10-0

Photograph: Cindy Momchilov

Cover: Natalie Alper, *October #1*, 1995, Cat. No. 7

Supported in part by the Arkansas Arts Council

Note: All dimensions are in inches. Height precedes width.

ARTISTS

RON ADAMS

NATALIE ALPER

ROBERT BRAWLEY

RODNEY CARSWELL

WILLIAM D. DAVIS

LESLEY DILL

CAROL HEPPER

DAVID HUFFMAN

ELISE KAUFMAN

IRA KORMAN

WHITFIELD LOVELL

TIM MOSMAN

STEPHEN NAMARA

HARVEY QUAYTMAN

Lenders to the exhibition:

George Adams Gallery, New York
Babcock Gallery, New York
Jan Baum Gallery, Los Angeles, California
Diane and Sandy Besser, Little Rock, Arkansas
Capricorn Galleries, Bethesda, Maryland
Susan Cummins Gallery, Mill Valley, California
Feigen, Incorporated, Chicago, Illinois
Jackye and Curtis Finch, Jr., Little Rock, Arkansas
Horwitch-LewAllen Gallery, Santa Fe, New Mexico
Koplin Gallery, Santa Monica, California
D. C. Moore Gallery, New York
Lucy and Paul Robinson, Little Rock, Arkansas
The Arkansas Arts Center Foundation

SIXTH NATIONAL DRAWING INVITATIONAL

Drawings reveal many things. They tell us about life and death, love and hate, comfort and suffering, stillness and light, the real and the imagined. They provide insight into the human condition. Works on paper are only limited by the soul, the mind, the hand and the experience of the maker. They make known what has laid fallow in the maker and hidden in the sheet; they make visual what has been secret, they release what has been contained. These revelations enrich our spirits; and we are moved and changed by the art we call drawing.

This Sixth National Drawing Invitational supports my contention that drawing today is as mysterious and as magical as the marks made on the walls of the Lascaux caves in France thousands and thousands of years ago. The need to release visual energy in order to convey what is seen, felt, known or unknown has driven artists to make drawings throughout history. This exhibition of the work of fourteen contemporary artists explores their concerns and interests. The fourteen have individual ideas, feelings and experiences that affect their approach to drawing. Each sees the world with different eyes, each has a different emotional concern, each has a different message to communicate, each treats the paper with a different touch. The strength of their differences and the power of what they as individuals have found hidden within themselves and released onto the sheets are what caused me to select their works for this exhibition.

Four different visions describe with penetrating insight the figure in isolation in the drawings by Ron Adams, Robert Brawley, Ira Korman and Stephen Namara.

Muscles that have labored and faces that know pain are reflected in two of the pen and ink works of Ron Adams. A transparent shirt drawn with flowing lines fails to hide the stress of the bodies of the woman and child in *Mulatto*, 1992. Detailed tonal cross hatching models the faces, hands and muscles as if cut from stone, expressing the anguish of being alone and forgotten. In *Dandelion Wine*, 1994, a story of a life past and present is made clear as a lone male figure attempts to transcend time while sitting with eyes closed, drinking wine and playing the guitar.

A brooding melancholy prevails in each of Ira Korman's charcoal drawings. In both *Paul,* 1992 and *Grandpa's Chair,* 1994, the figure is cloaked in the overall darkness of the sheet. Light describes sullen forms, skin and fabric texture. *Sweet Virginia,* 1994, has a more even light throughout the composition which emphasizes the folds of the blanket, the wrinkles of the pillows and the fatigue of the resting woman. In each of these works the slightly diagonal placement of the image furthers the shadowy mystery.

Graphite is used to create a silvery glow to the haunting quality of the compositions of Robert Brawley. In the delicate drawing, *Young Woman Listening to Music,* 1994, a symmetrical composition reinforces the serenity of the mood of the slouching figure—her shirt open, her soul open also to the transforming sounds she is hearing. An intense, straightforward placement and gaze, coupled with a more crisp treatment of the graphite, set an eerie mood to both *Portrait of Morgan,* 1991-92, and *Study in Gray, Nude #2,* 1993.

There is a sense of surprise and uncertainty captured with the figure drawings by Stephen Namara. The sensuous charcoal and chalk, *Female Model,* 1993, arms raised and covering the face, uses gentle tone and delicate searching lines to show the movement and beauty of the form. In *Adelle,* 1994, the sitting frontal figure is bolder; heavier lines and deeper shadows are used, particularly in the surprised-looking face and eyes. The orange dry pigment of the headwrap and torso garment adds a surreal quality to the work. In the colorful *Untitled,* 1995, sudden shock is clear in the expression of the woman as she glares out and grasps her breast.

Lyrical movement of line, shapes and color fill the moody and poetic compositions of Natalie Alper, Carol Hepper and Tim Mosman.

A haunting silence much like the atmosphere before a tornado is disrupted with curving, imposing lines in the mixed media drawings of Natalie Alper. The energy springs from a dark form on the lower right in *January #4,* 1994, moving with light and dark curving lines upward and off the sheet, freezing for us a vanishing melody. The beauty of the song is more constant in the layered movement of the sounds from the lines and forms in *August #3*, 1995. In *October 1*, 1995, Alper builds the notes from the bottom of the sheet to a robust, reverberating conclusion of joy at the top.

Carol Hepper choreographs the motion of forms on the paper, creating a ballet of sizes and shapes. The forms that move about appear to be organic or structural in nature. In the two *Untitled* drawings of 1993, the forms seem to float or blow with the wind in constant flux, leaving an afterimage of joy. More control directs the movement and direction of shapes in *Untitled*, 1995. In this work, texture and connections add to the complexity of the spatial and fluid surreal ballet.

Dark lines emerge from the gray-blue ground much like noises in the night in the acrylic works on paper by Tim Mosman. Out of the grayness of the sheet in *Loss of Identity*, 1995, lines grow into shapes which seem to move, then rest, then move again, their size and shape changing the space they occupy. The effect is that of a symphony, with sounds coming and going from different sections to form a harmony. *Untitled #195073*, 1995, is more organic, with the lines growing from the page into plantlike shapes that vary from delicate substances to bold masses.

Structure, geometry and space help define the vision and the work of Elise Kaufman, Rodney Carswell and Harvey Quaytman.

An architectural blueprint is the ground or sheet that Elise Kaufman uses to begin her work, *All Fall Down*, 1994. On this very ordered structure she introduces lines, tones and shapes to articulate her drawing with personal elements. Energy is created with a falling cube and square as well as with dots, smudges and color which cause the composition to move and hold together. Isolation is established in *Cabin Fever*, 1994, by a division of space and placement of the house image. The isolation is furthered by the containment of the words "Cabin Fever" and by the three picture planes. *Cabin Fever, 2*, 1995, reflects the explosive nature of restriction.

Rodney Carswell uses flat, geometric shapes to

generate spatial energy and relationship in his *Untitled*, 1989. Two overlapping rectangles of silver-gray dominate a smaller receding panel of red. The distance between the two forms seems to change as does the surface of the gray shape containing a cross shape. Translucent color is used as overlapping planes in *Untitled*, 1990. The surface is bound by a linear grid of various widths which creates a complex illusion of space. Varying sizes of rectangular shapes cause the surface of *Untitled*, 1994, to pulsate with constant change.

Surfaces which have been built up and caressed with color and tone impart a sensuous quality to the geometric drawings of Harvey Quaytman. In both *First Drawing*, 1995, and *Wismuth*, 1995, a vertical and horizontal shape form a cross to divide the golden space. In *First Drawing*, the cross shape is quite thin and the surface has color changes, suggesting varying texture in each of the resulting quadrants. The cross in *Wismuth* is dominating the composition because of the width and the built-up edges of the cross. *Bister*, 1994, is much more complex, with shifting planes of color moving from right to left as well as up and down. Each work creates its own energy because of the size and placement of geometric forms and the surface variation.

David Huffman, Whitfield Lovell, William Davis and Lesley Dill use astonishing images to express strong and compelling statements about their world.

Feels Like Fire, 1994, is David Huffman's portrait about love. With acrylic and color pencil on cardboard he shapes a pensive face—moon eyed and dreamy, but strong and determined in his quest. He adds the words in case there is doubt about the meaning of *Feels Like Fire*. Enthusiastic words, lines and color describe a love dance and exchange of difficulty as well as joy in *Rebel Kiss*, 1995. Built up lines find facial form and human emotion in the explosive *Africanus*, 1995.

Whitfield Lovell reveals his history with symbolic icons on a grand scale. The dreamlike image of the folded hands, the dress with the tree anchored in the center of the picture plane, in *Dress with Tree*, 1992, tells us about the strength of prayer, the tree of life and the power of what has come before. *Hand II*, 1994, and *Hand XIII*, 1995, majestically illustrate the forces of the right and left hand on our lives and on the people held in those hands. The images are drawn with grace and devotion.

Symbolism, dreams and fantasy are the kingdom of William Davis. He draws with such surety and beauty that he convinces us in each work that he not only has observed each tale but that he knows each player and object. In *Shaman's Table*, 1987, the dragon and jester are in full control of the dance as we are asked to join the tight composition for the party. In both *St. George, Dino and March Meet the Fool*, 1992, and *Mumbletypeg and Other Games Boys Play*, 1986-94, we are carried back to medieval and gothic days of horror and delight. Each inch of the drawings is full of intrigue and wonder.

The figure in the work of Lesley Dill embodies the hopes as well as the anguish of life. It also serves as the carrier of the poetry of Emily Dickinson. The nude torso (soul) emerges from the darkness of the past, bearing the haunting poetry as part of itself in *Untitled (The Soul Has Bandaged Moments...)*, 1994. In *Poem Thread Figure (White)*, 1995, the words of Dickinson again are the substance and meaning of the figure. While the threads might have hidden them in the past, they conceal them no longer. The struggle of the words and the flesh for liberation reach their climax in the monumental, *A Word Made Flesh*, 1995.

The compelling statements on paper made by these fourteen artists reveal what their makers know about yesterday, today and tomorrow. Feelings and thoughts have been liberated from within and made visible for us to contemplate, understand and enjoy. The results are as diverse and varied in content as we who apprehend them are diverse and varied. They touch our minds and our souls in different ways; they speak of our sameness even as they speak about our uniqueness. They are the truths—and perhaps the beauty—of their makers. They are the art we call drawings.

Townsend Wolfe
1996

RON ADAMS

Born 1934 in Detroit, Michigan, lives in Santa Fe, New Mexico

Selected Collections:
Albuquerque Museum of Art, History & Science, New Mexico
Bronx Museum of the Arts, New York
California Afro-American Museum, Los Angeles
Hampton University, University Museum, Virginia
Museum of New Mexico, Santa Fe
National Museum of American Art, Washington, D.C.
The Arkansas Arts Center Foundation

Selected Exhibitions:
1995 *African American Works from the Permanent Collection,* The Arkansas Arts Center
1991 Eastern New Mexico University, Portales (solo)
1990 College of Santa Fe, New Mexico
1987 Fine Arts Museum, Santa Fe, New Mexico
1986 *62nd Annual Prints Competition*, Society of American Graphic Artists, New York
Taos Arts Association/Stables Art Center, New Mexico

1. *Mulatto*, 1992
   ink on paper
   57 x 49 inches
   The Arkansas Arts Center
   Foundation Collection:
   The '94 Tabriz Fund. 92.57

2. *Rorschach Riddle*, 1992
   mixed media on paper
   42 1/2 x 27 1/2 inches

3. *Dandelion Wine*, 1994
   pen and ink on paper
   50 x 38 inches

   Lent by Horwitch-LewAllen
   Gallery, Santa Fe, New Mexico.

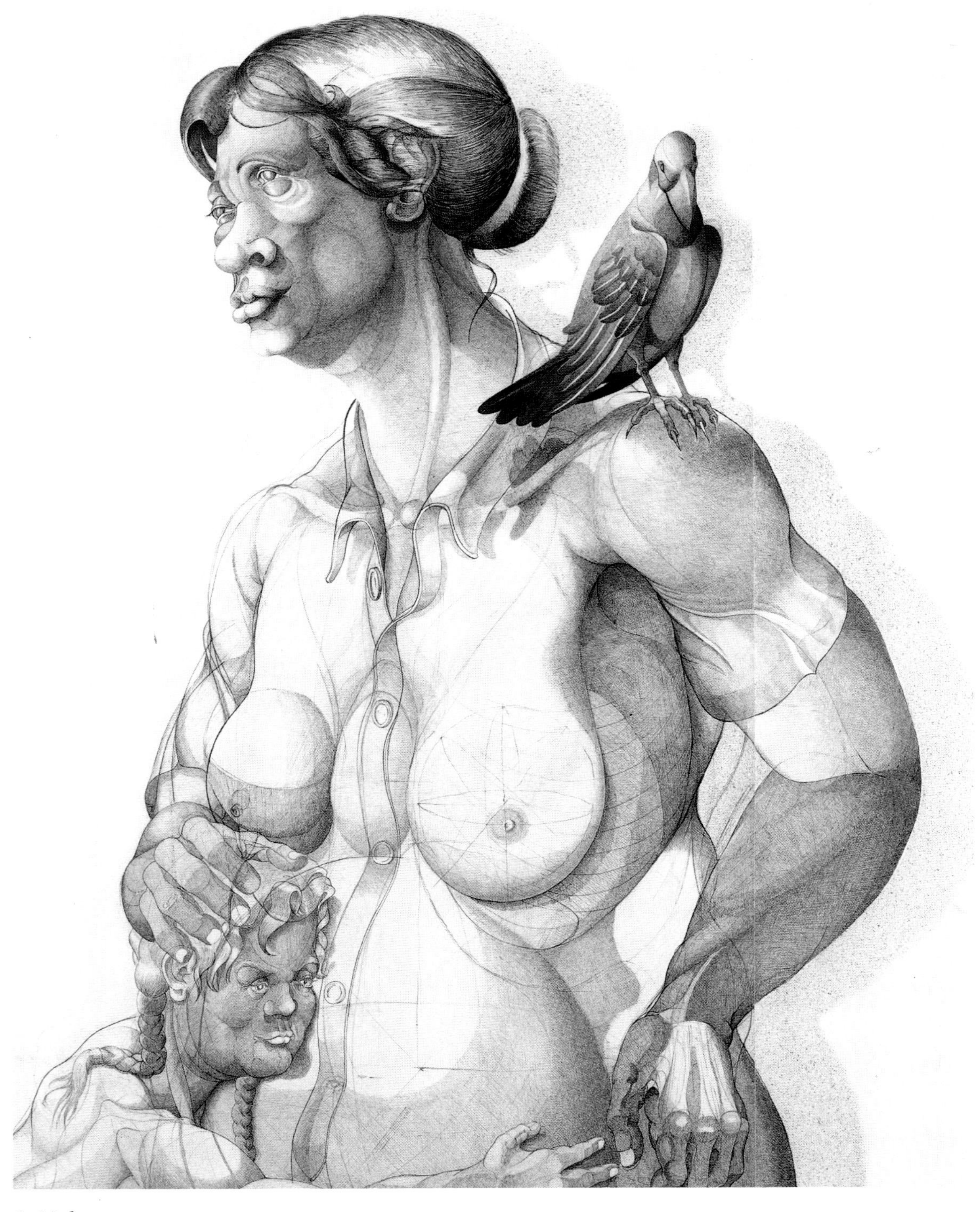

1. *Mulatto*

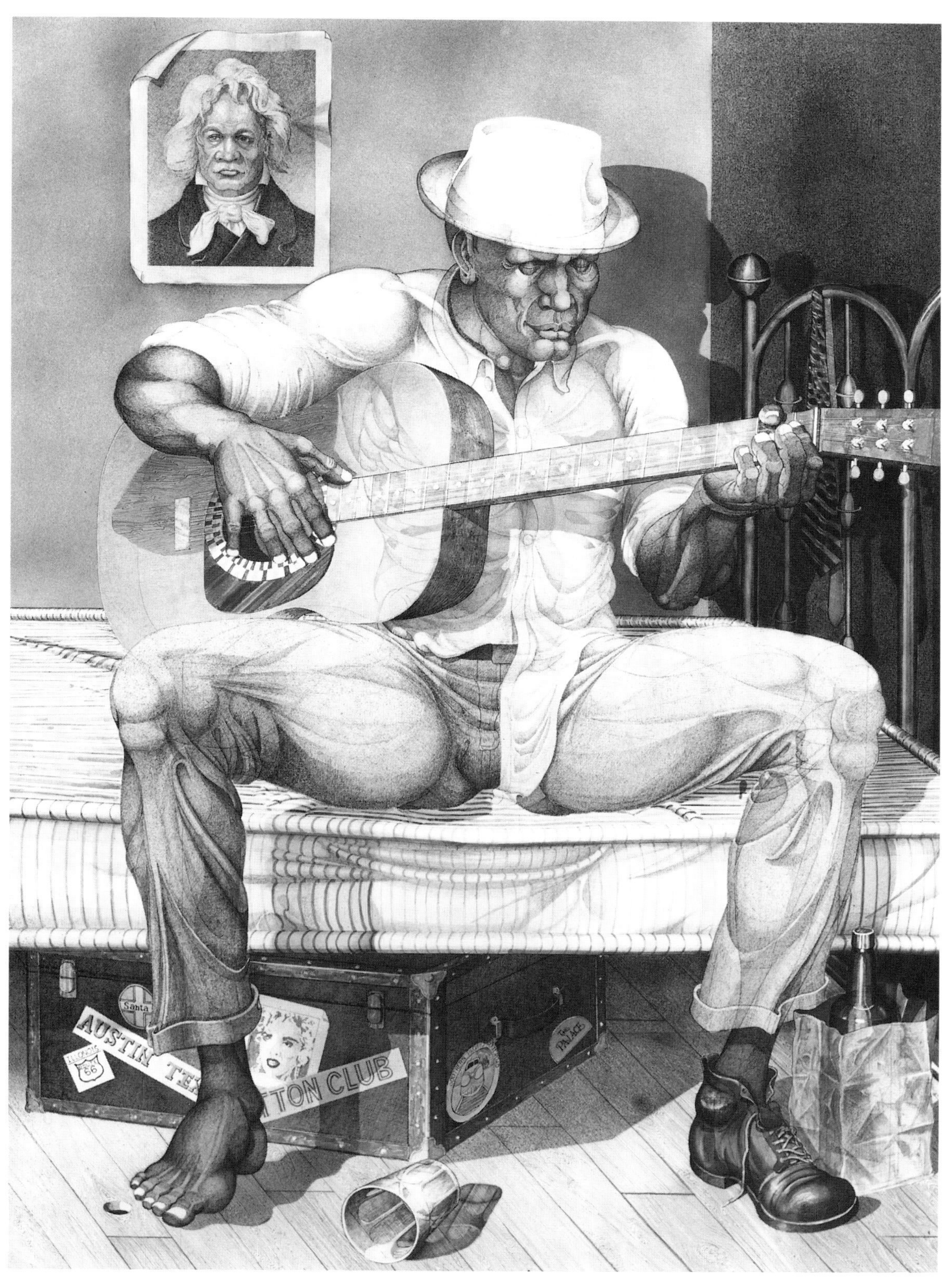

3. *Dandelion Wine*

NATALIE ALPER

Born 1942 in the Bronx, New York, lives in Brookline, Massachusetts
Education: M.A. Boston University, Massachusetts
M.A. School of the Museum of Fine Arts, Boston, Massachusetts
B.A. New York University, Washington Square College

Selected Collections:
Addison Gallery of American Art, Phillips Academy, Andover, Massachusetts
Fine Arts Museums of San Francisco, Achenbach Foundation for the Graphic Arts, California
Harvard University Art Museums, William Hayes Fogg Art Museum, Cambridge, Massachusetts
Massachusetts Institute of Technology, Cambridge
Museum of Fine Arts, Boston, Massachusetts
National Museum of American Art, Smithsonian Institution, Washington, D.C.
The Phillips Collection, Washington, D.C.

Selected Exhibitions:
1995 Howard Yezerski Gallery, Boston, Massachusetts (solo)
1994 Margaret Lipworth Fine Arts, Boca Raton, Florida (solo)
Howard Yezerski Gallery, Boston, Massachusetts (solo)
1992 Howard Yezerski Gallery, Boston, Massachusetts (solo)
1991 de Andino Fine Arts, Washington, D.C. (solo)
American Abstraction at the Addison, Addison Gallery of Art, Phillips Academy, Andover, Massachusetts
1989 Addison Gallery of American Art, Phillips Academy, Andover, Massachusetts (solo)

4. *January #4*, 1994
mixed media, metallic pigment on paper
22 x 15 inches

5. *June #2*, 1995
mixed media, metallic pigment on paper
22 x 15 inches

6. *August #3*, 1995
mixed media, metallic pigment on paper
22 x 15 inches
Arkansas Arts Center Foundation Purchase, 1996.

7. *October #1*, 1995
mixed media, metallic pigment on paper
22 x 15 inches

Lent by the artist.

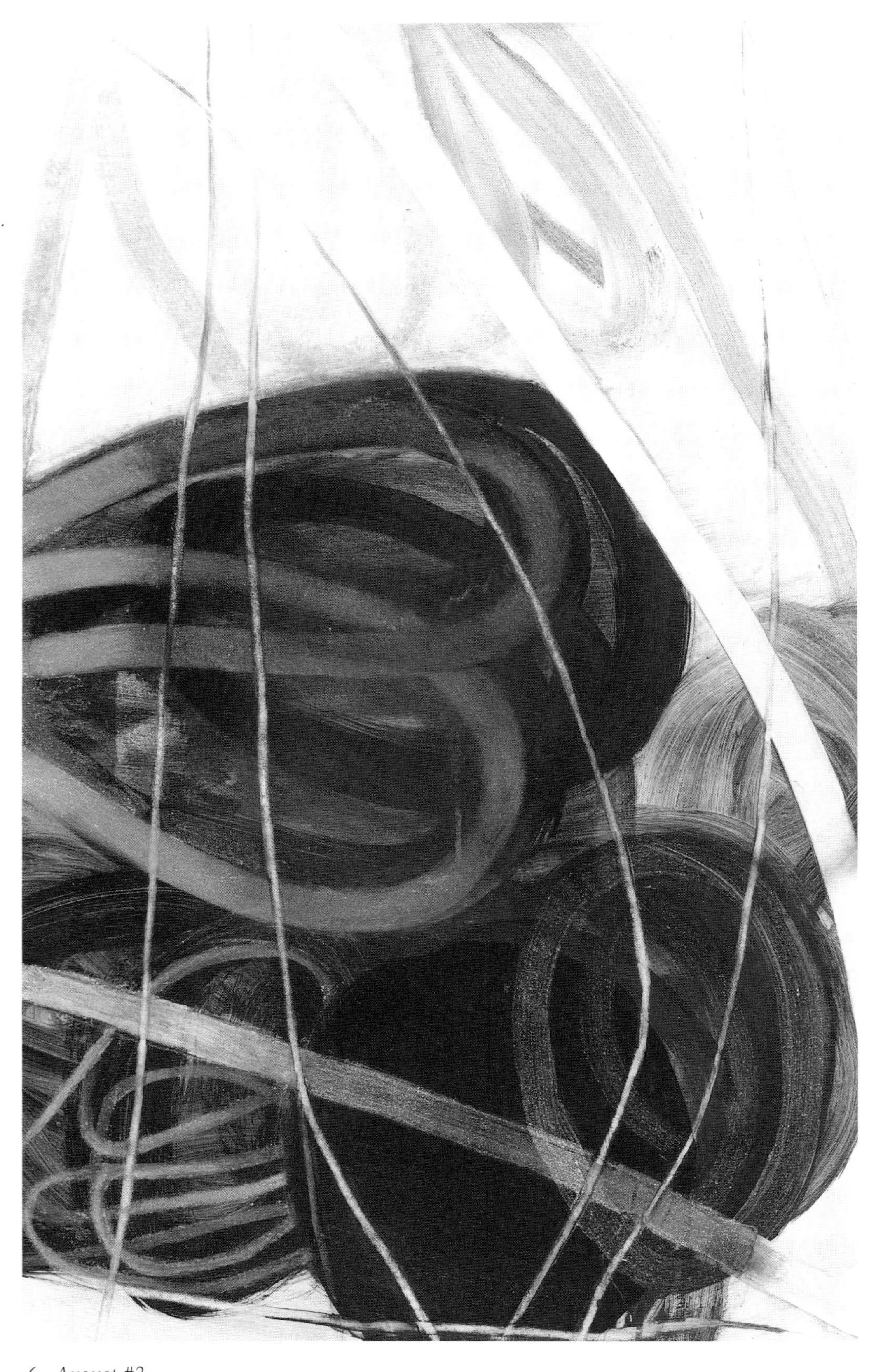

6. *August #3*

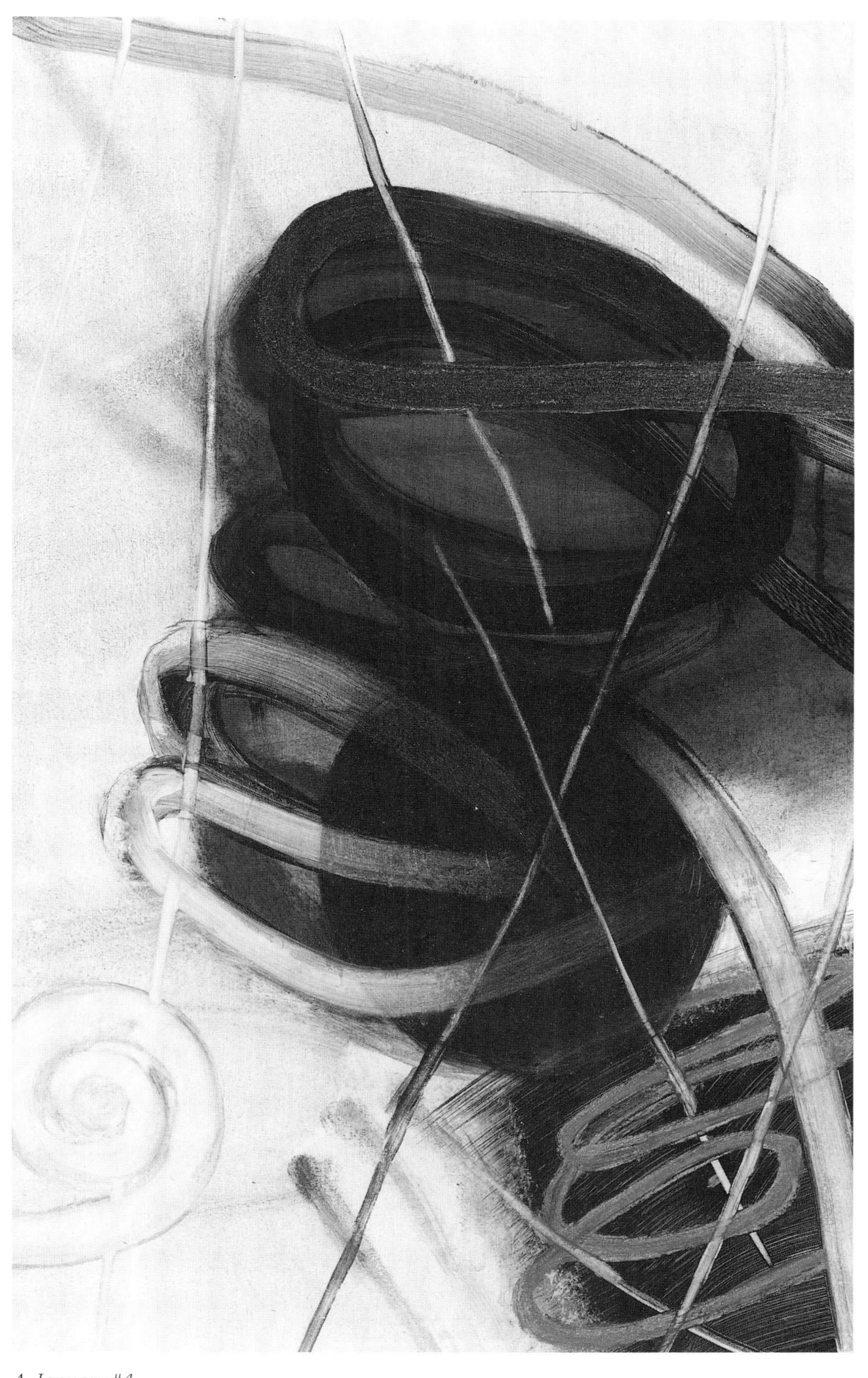

4. *January #4*

ROBERT BRAWLEY

Born 1937 in Brainerd, Minnesota, lives in Concord, California
Education: M.F.A., 1965, San Francisco Art Institute, California
B.A., 1963, San Francisco Art Institute, California

Selected Collections:
The Art Institute of Chicago, Illinois
Hoyt Institute of Fine Arts, New Castle, Pennsylvania
National Museum of American Art, Smithsonian Institution, Washington, D.C.
Nelson-Atkins Museum of Art, Kansas City, Missouri
San Francisco Art Institute, California
The Arkansas Arts Center Foundation

Selected Exhibitions:
1982 *The New Realists*, Mongerson Galleries, Chicago, Illinois
Hoyt National Painting Show, Hoyt Institute of Fine Arts, New Castle, Pennsylvania
Mid Year National Exhibition, Butler Institute of American Art, Youngstown, Ohio
Small Works Exhibition, New York University, New York
1971 *San Francisco New Realism - Through the Photograph to Painting*, San Francisco Museum of Art, California

8. *Portrait of Morgan*, 1991-92
graphite on paper
46 x 35 inches
Lent by Capricorn Galleries, Bethesda, Maryland.

9. *Study in Gray, Nude #2*, 1993
graphite on paper
23 x 23 inches
Arkansas Arts Center Foundation Purchase, Collections Group Fund, 1996.

10. *Young Woman Listening to Music*, 1994
graphite on paper
22 x 20 inches
Arkansas Arts Center Foundation Purchase, 1996.

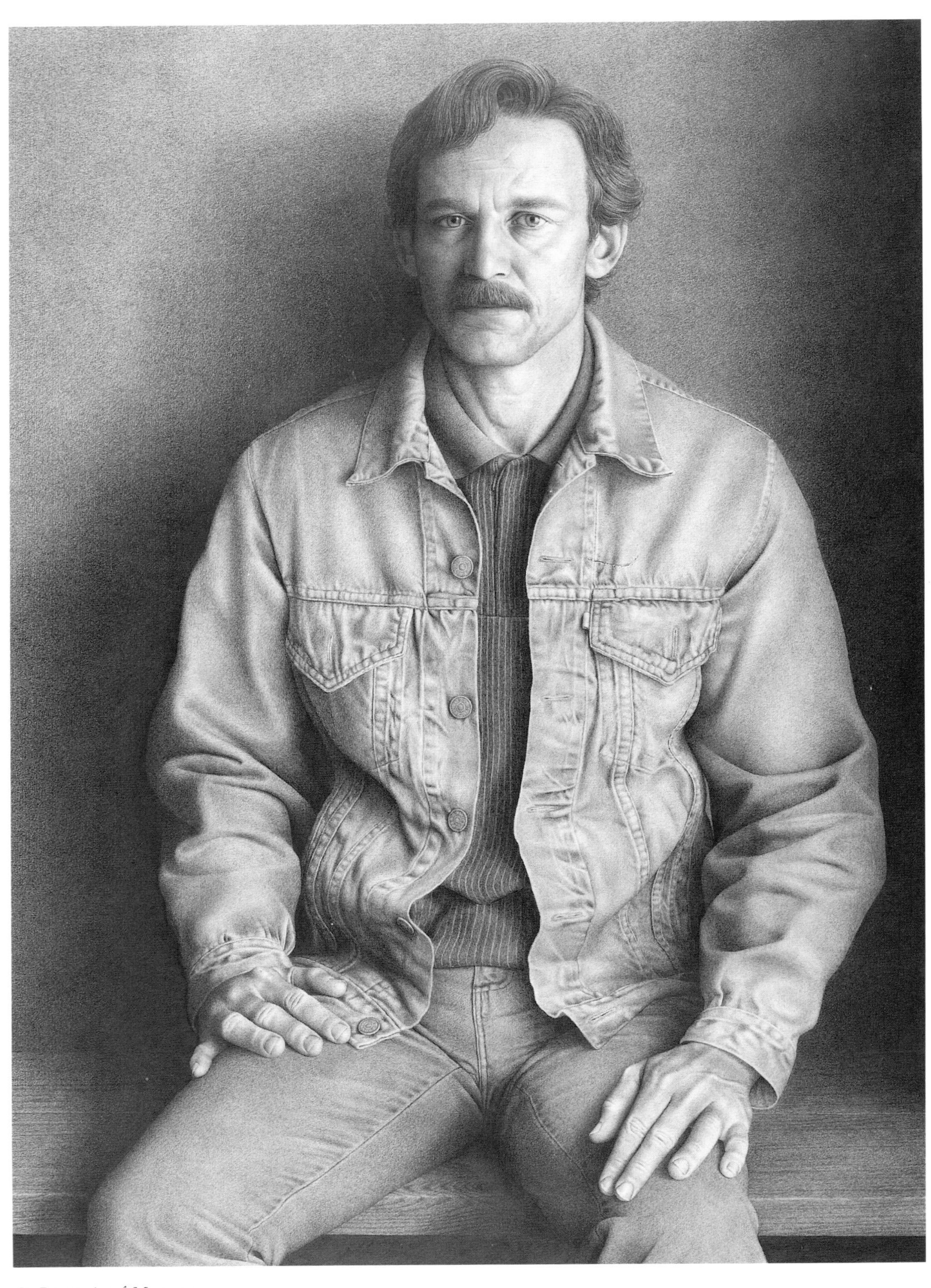

8. *Portrait of Morgan*

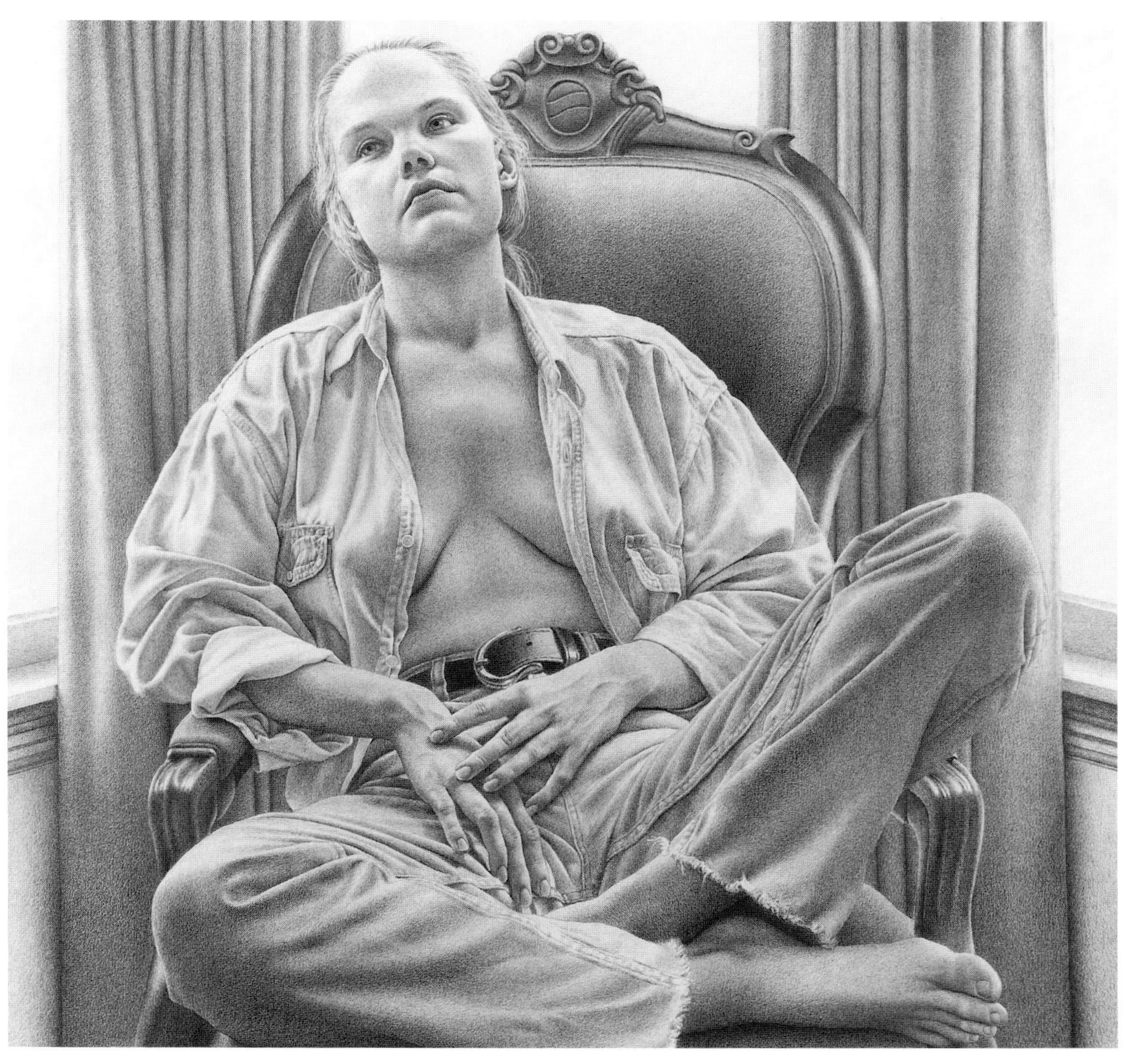

10. *Young Woman Listening to Music*

RODNEY CARSWELL

Born 1946 in Carmel, California, lives in Chicago, Illinois
Education: M.F.A., 1972, University of Colorado, Boulder
B.F.A., 1968, University of New Mexico, Albuquerque

Selected Collections:
The Art Institute of Chicago, Illinois
Art Museum, University of New Mexico, Albuquerque
Columbia Pictures, Los Angeles, California
Illinois State Museum, Springfield
University of Colorado, Boulder
University of Oklahoma, Fred Jones Jr. Museum of Art, Norman
The Arkansas Arts Center Foundation

Selected Exhibitions:
1995 Feigen, Inc., Chicago, Illinois (solo)
44th Biennial Exhibition of Contemporary Painting: Painting Outside Painting, The Corcoran Gallery of Art, Washington, D.C.
Chicago Abstract Paintings, Evanston Art Center, Illinois
1994 *The Content of Abstraction*, Arts Center College of DuPage, Glen Ellyn, Illinois
1993 Renaissance Society, Chicago, Illinois (solo, catalogue)
1992 Linda Durham Gallery, Santa Fe, New Mexico (solo)
Roy Boyd Gallery, Chicago, Illinois (solo)
New Acquisitions, Illinois State Museum, Springfield
New Acquisitions, Mulvane Art Museum, Topeka, Kansas

11. *Untitled*, 1989
acrylic on paper
22 1/2 x 22 inches
Arkansas Arts Center
Foundation Purchase, 1989.
89.57

12. *Untitled*, 1990
acrylic on paper
60 x 40 inches

13. *Untitled*, 1994
acrylic on paper
30 1/4 x 22 1/4 inches

Lent by Feigen, Incorporated, Chicago, Illinois.

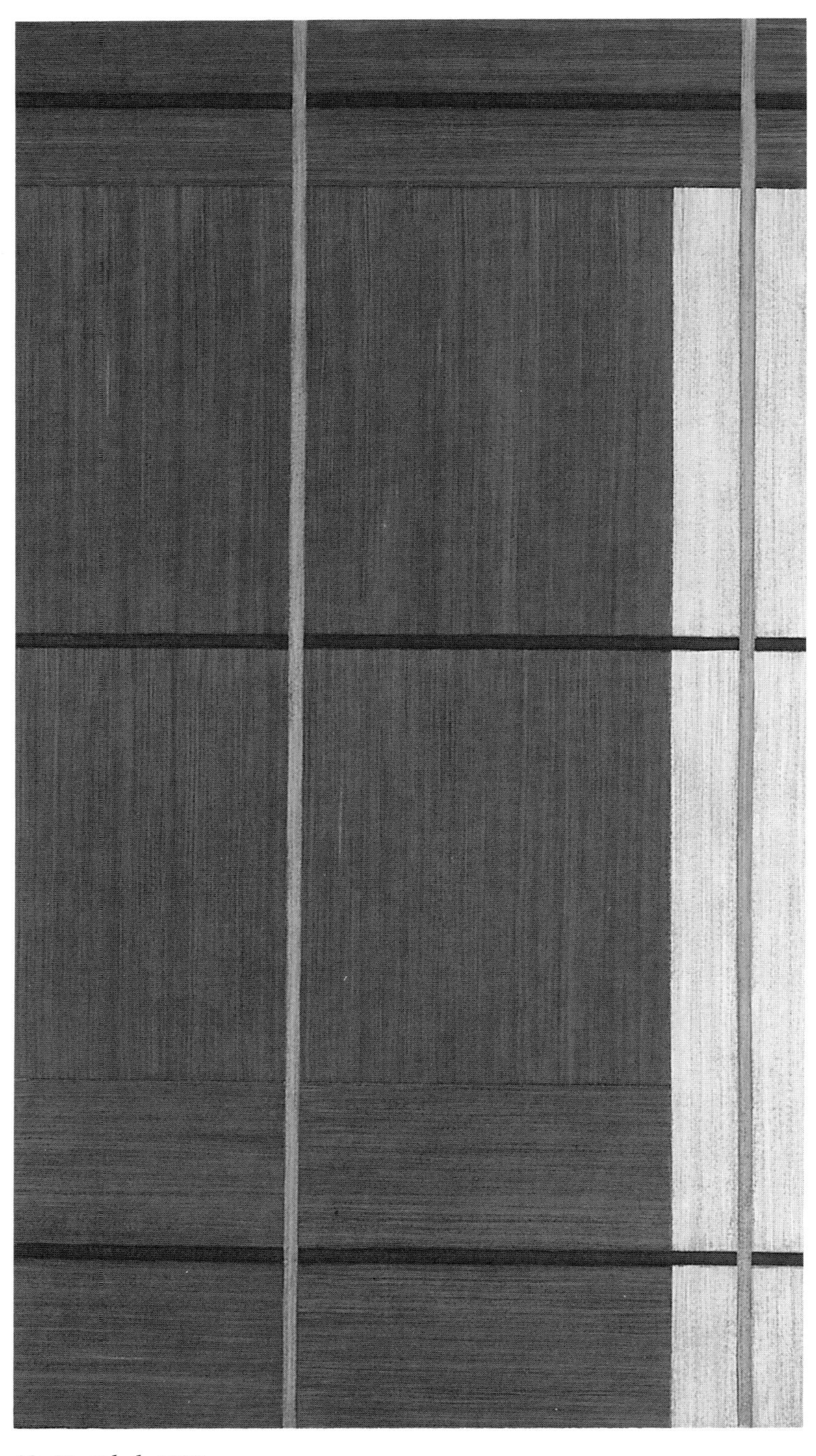

12. *Untitled, 1990*

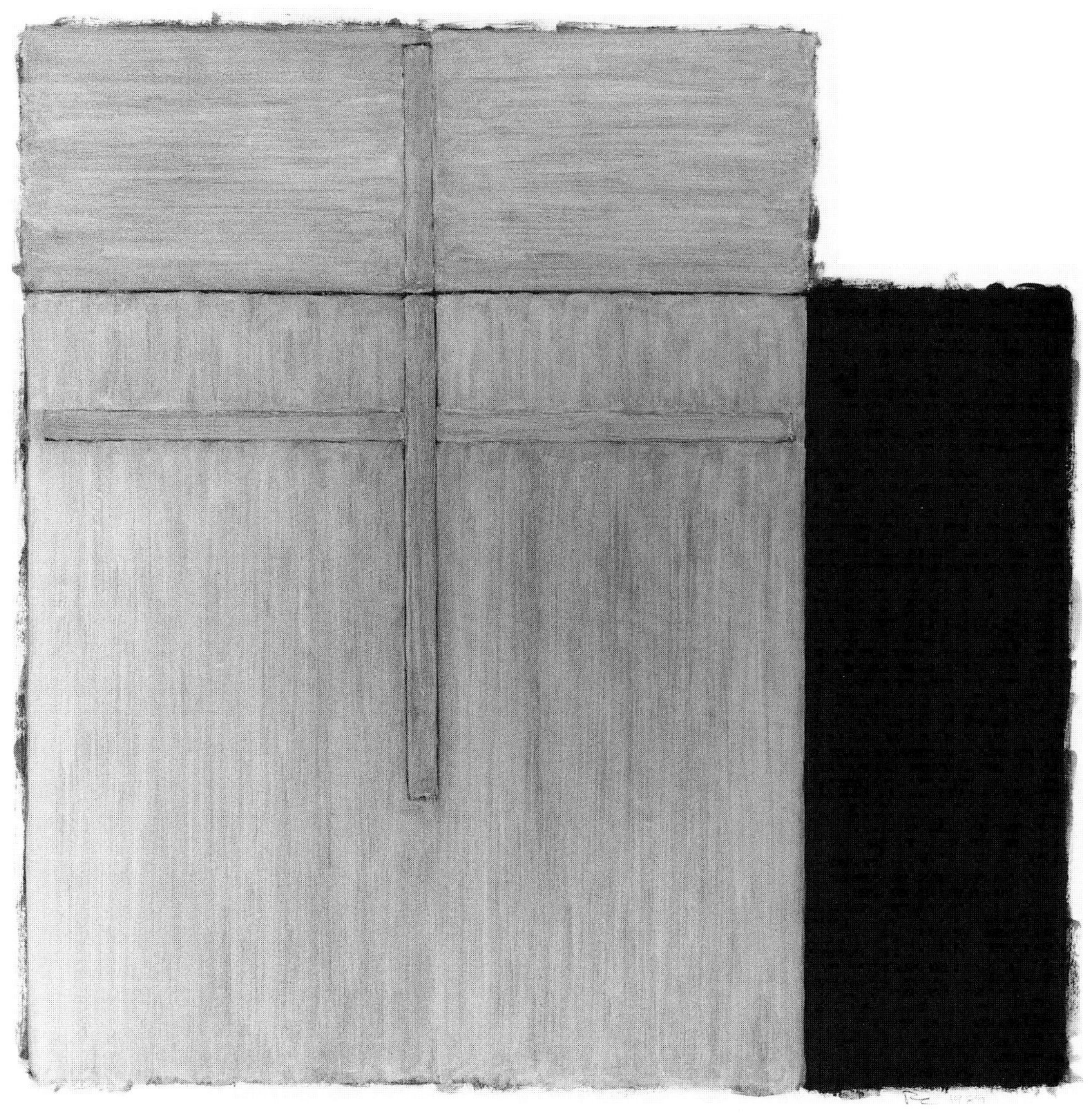

11. *Untitled, 1989*

WILLIAM D. DAVIS

Born 1936 in Erie, Pennsylvania, lives in Shippensburg
Education: M.F.A., 1980, Pennsylvania State University, University Park
B.S., 1959, Edinboro State College, Warren, Pennsylvania

Selected Collections:
Bruce Gallery, Edinboro University of Pennsylvania, Edinboro
Kipp Gallery, Indiana University of Pennsylvania, Indiana, Pennsylvania
Lock Haven University, Pennsylvania
Milton Shoe Collection Contemporary American Prints & Drawings, Pennsylvania
Hazel Sandford Gallery, Clarion University, Clarion, Pennsylvania

Selected Exhibitions:
1995 Bald Eagle National Biennial Invitational, Williamsport, Pennsylvania
Chatauqua National Juried Exhibition, Chautauqua, New York
1994 National Academy of Design, New York
Austin Peay State University, Clarksville, Tennessee
1993 West Georgia College, Carrolton, Georgia (solo)
Southern Alleghenies Triennial Invitational, Loretto, Pennsylvania
1990 Doshi Center for Contemporary Art, Harrisburg, Pennsylvania

14. *Shaman's Table*, 1987
graphite on paper
28 x 37 inches

15. *St. George, Dino, and Mardi Meet the Fool*, 1992
graphite on paper
37 x 28 inches
Arkansas Arts Center
Foundation Purchase, 1996.

16. *Mumbletypeg and Other Games Boys Play*, 1986-94
graphite on paper
39 x 28 1/2 inches

Lent by Babcock Gallery, New York.

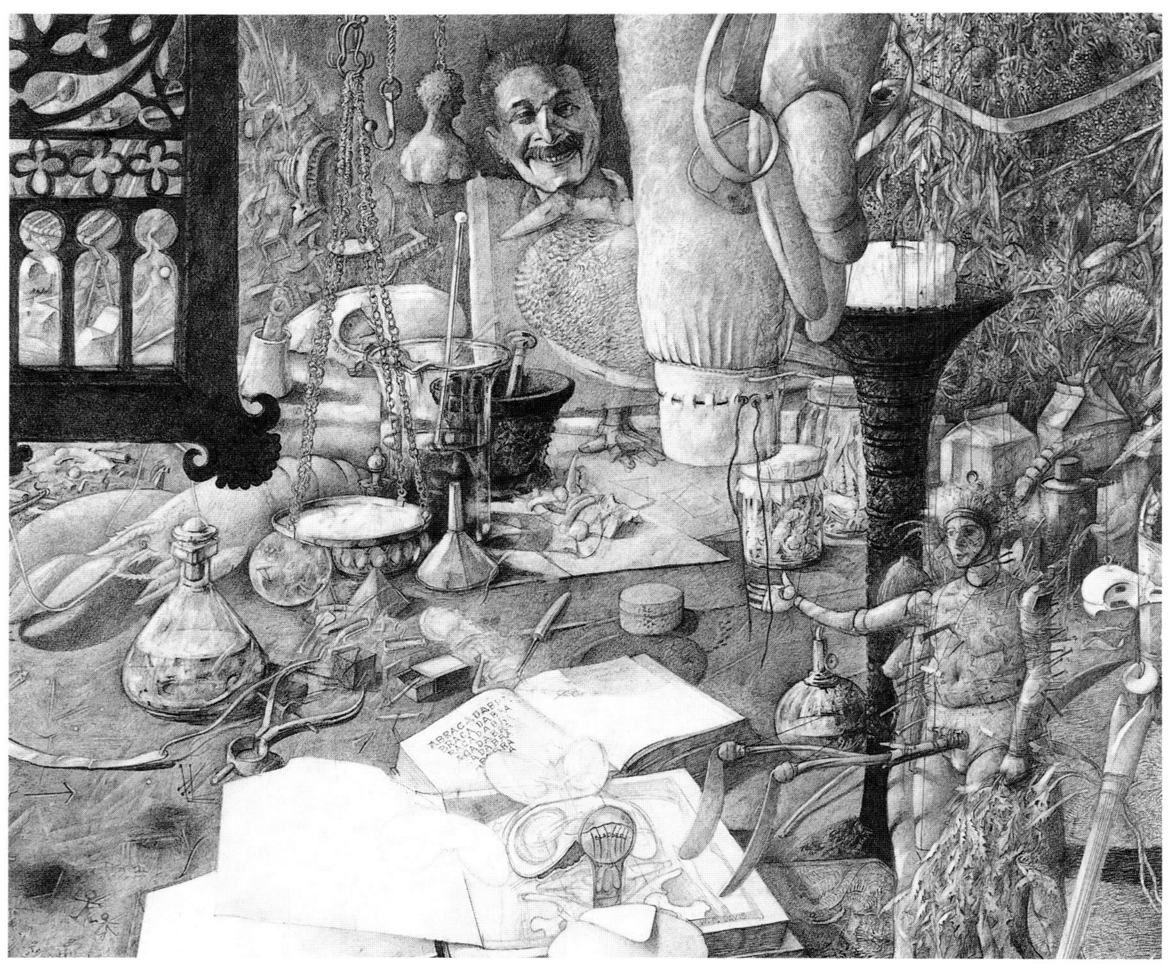

14. *Shaman's Table*

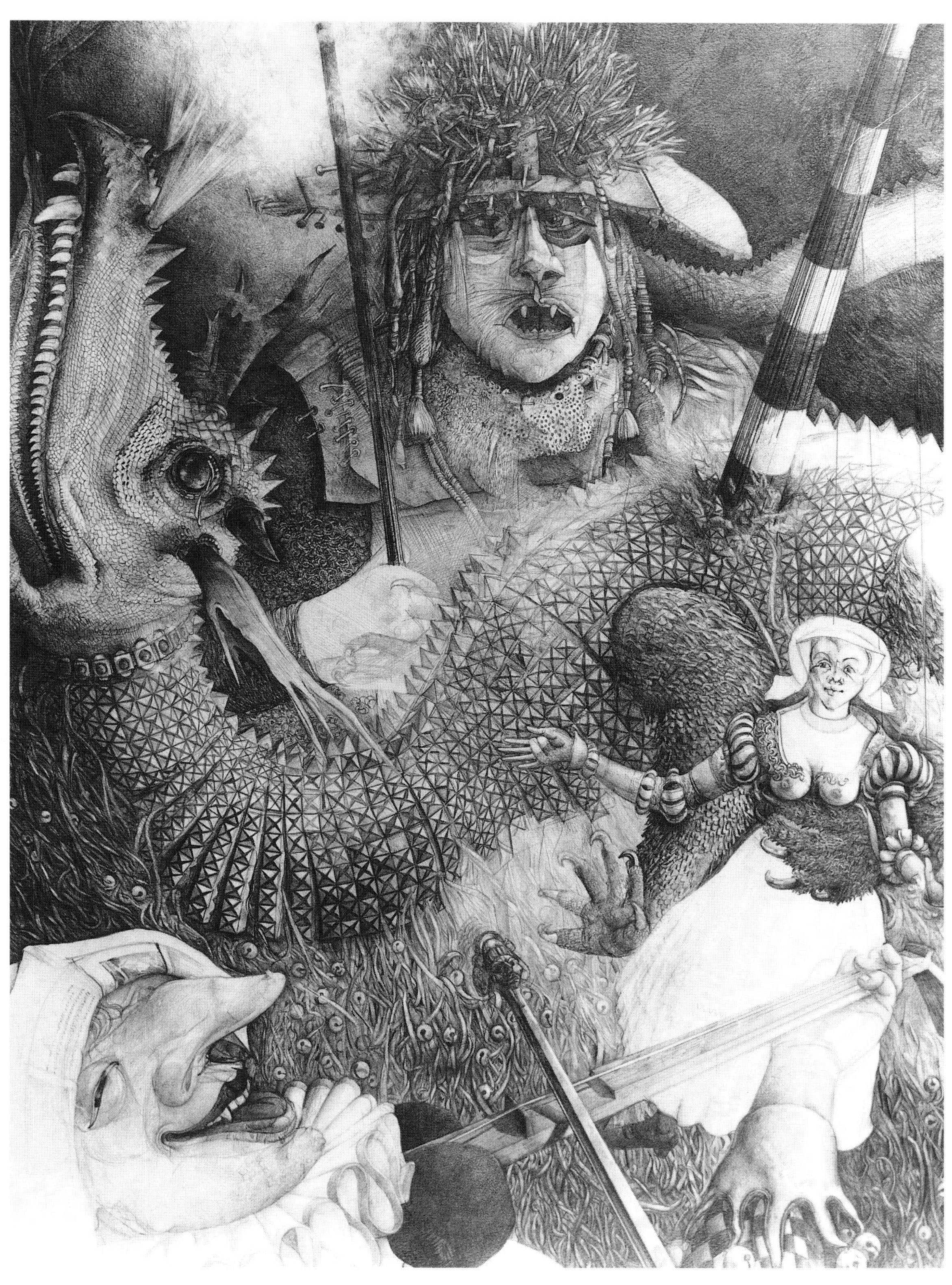

15. *St. George, Dino, and Mardi Meet the Fool*

LESLEY DILL

Born 1950 in Bronxville, New York, lives in New York
Education: M.F.A., 1980, Maryland Institute of Art, Baltimore
M.A.. 1974, Smith College, Northampton, Massachusetts
B.A., 1972, Trinity College, Hartford, Connecticut

Selected Collections:
Achenbach Foundation, M. H. de Young Memorial Museum, San Francisco, California
Florida International University, Miami
The Metropolitan Museum of Art, New York
Munson-Williams-Proctor Institute, Utica, New York
Museum of Modern Art, New York
Orlando Museum of Art, Florida
Whitney Museum of American Art, New York
The Arkansas Arts Center Foundation

Selected Exhibitions:
1995 *Voices in My Head*, George Adams Gallery, New York (solo)
Lesley Dill: An Installation, Gallery at Dieu Donne Papermill, New York (solo)
The Outer Layer, New Jersey Center for Visual Arts, Summit, New Jersey
Hudson Valley Artists '95: Domestic Policies, The College Art Gallery at New Paltz, New York
Reinventing the Emblem, Yale University Art Gallery, New Haven, Connecticut
1994 *5 Women Sculptors*, sponsored by Organization of Independent Artists at XI Valparalso Bienal, Chile
Works for Young Collectors, The Lemberg Gallery, St. Louis, Missouri
1993 *The Poetic Body*, Bernard Toale Gallery, Boston, Massachusetts (solo)

17. *Untitled (The Soul Has Bandaged Moments...)*, 1994
charcoal on paper
73 x 48 inches
The Arkansas Arts Center Foundation Collection:
The '94 Tabriz Fund. 95.8

18. *Poem Thread Figure (White)*, 1995
oil paint, thread on photograph
19 3/4 x 16 inches

19. *A Word Made Flesh*, 1995
oilstick, gold leaf, thread, butcher's wax on archival photo fiber paper
74 x 36 inches

Lent by George Adams Gallery, New York.

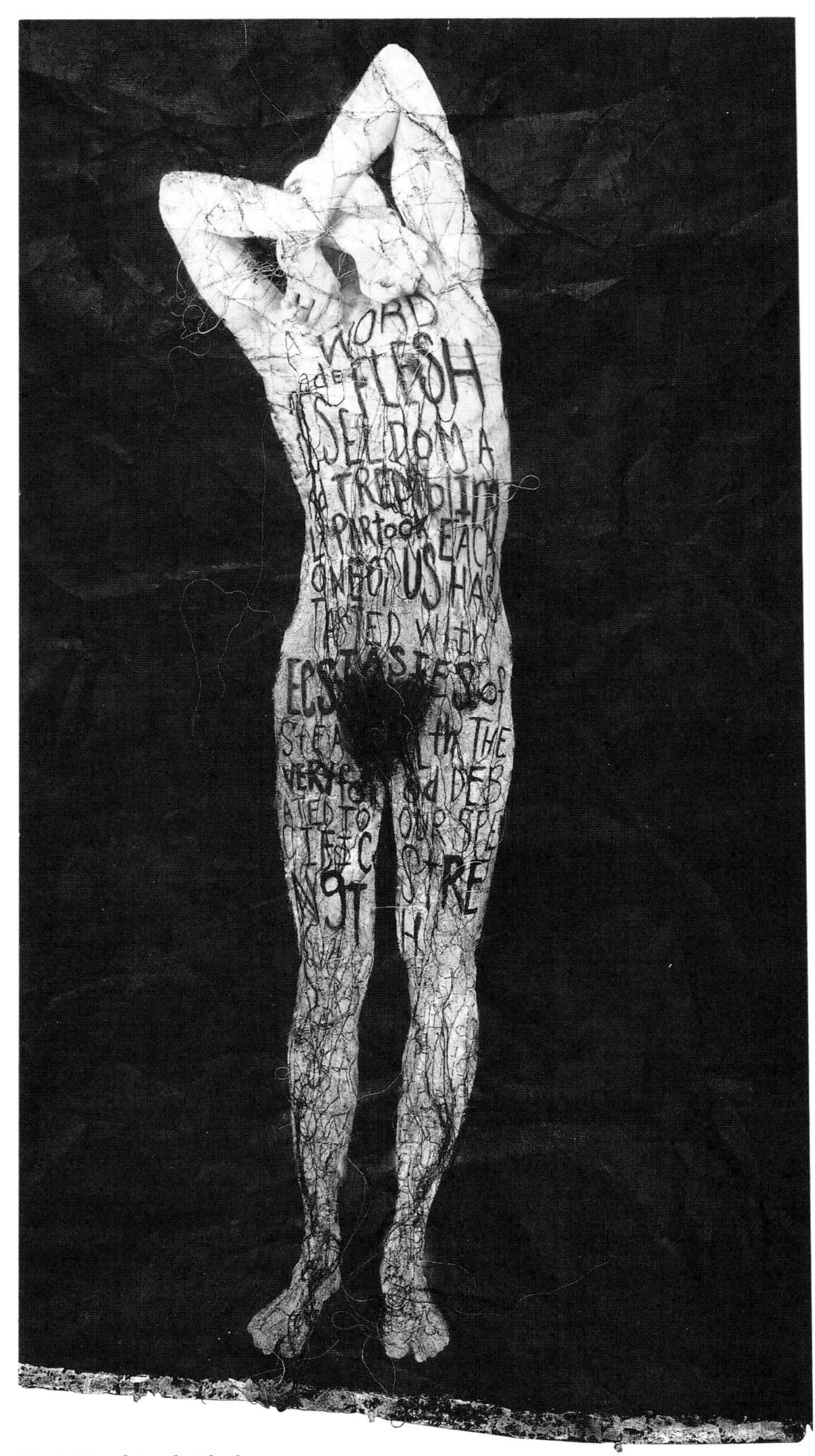

19. *A Word Made Flesh*

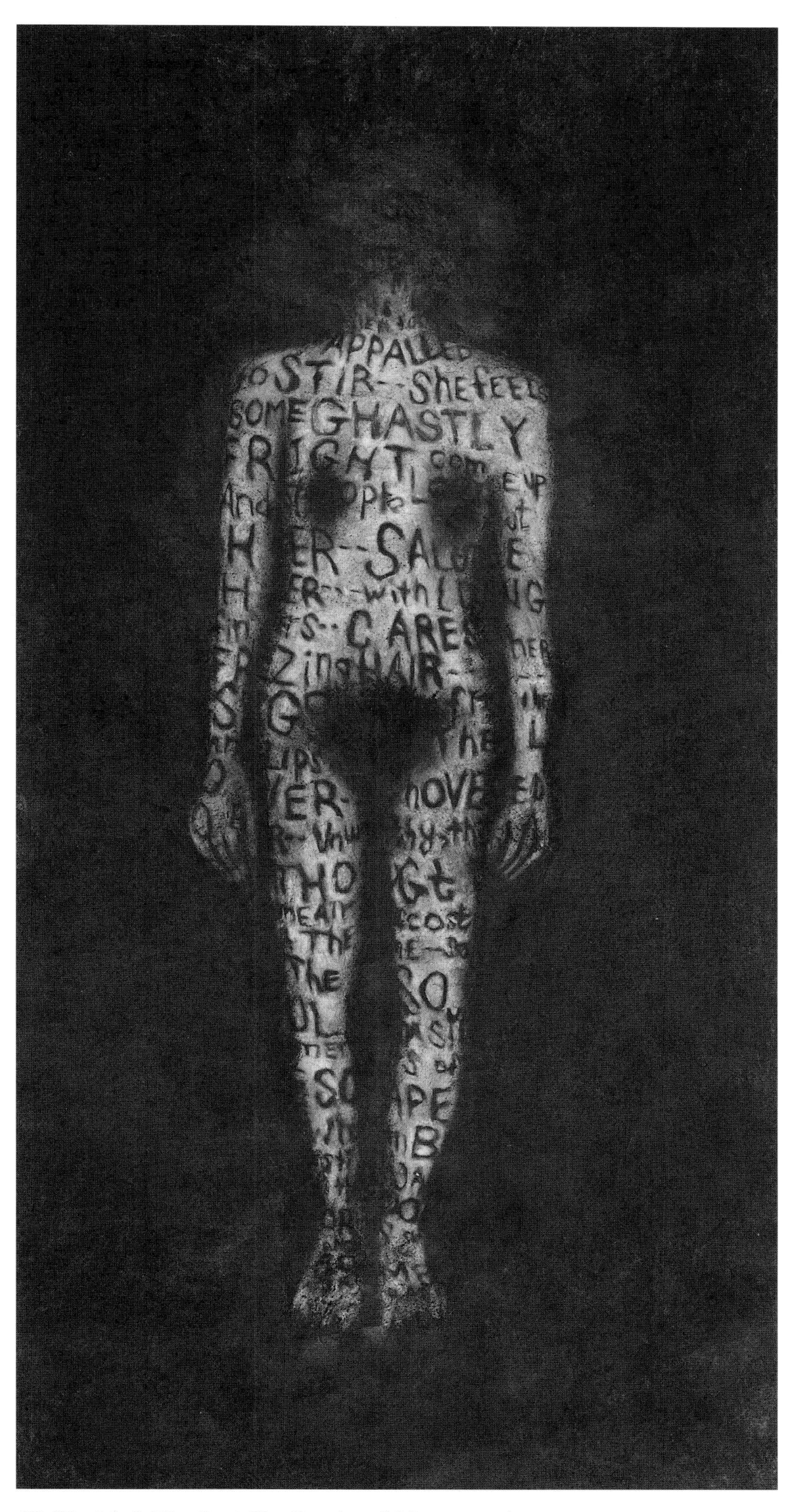

17. *Untitled (The Soul Has Bandaged Moments...)*

CAROL HEPPER

Born 1953 in McLaughlin, South Dakota, lives in New York
Education: B.S., 1975, South Dakota State University, Brookings

Selected Collections:
Detroit Institute of Arts, Michigan
Laumeier Sculpture Park, St. Louis, Missouri
The Metropolitan Museum of Art, New York
The Newark Museum, New Jersey
Orlando Museum of Art, Florida
Solomon R. Guggenheim Museum, New York
Walker Art Center, Minneapolis, Minnesota

Selected Exhibitions:
1995 *Twentieth Century American Sculpture at the White House,* Washington, D.C.
1995 *Work in Progress,* Mississippi Museum of Art, Mississippi (solo)
1995 Elizabeth Leach Gallery, Portland, Oregon (solo)
1994 Hartman & Company, LaJolla, California (solo)
1994 Michael Lord Gallery, Milwaukee, Wisconsin (solo)
1993 Galerie Waltraud Matt, Eschen, Liechtenstein (solo)
1992 Worcester Art Museum, Massachusetts (solo)

20. *Untitled,* 1993
gouache and pencil on paper
26 x 19 inches

21. *Untitled,* 1993
gouache, pencil, and charcoal on paper
26 x 19 inches

22. *Connective Tissue,* 1995
inks on parchment
35 x 16 1/2 inches

23. *Untitled,* 1995
gouache, conte, and pencil on paper
41 x 25 inches

Lent by the artist.

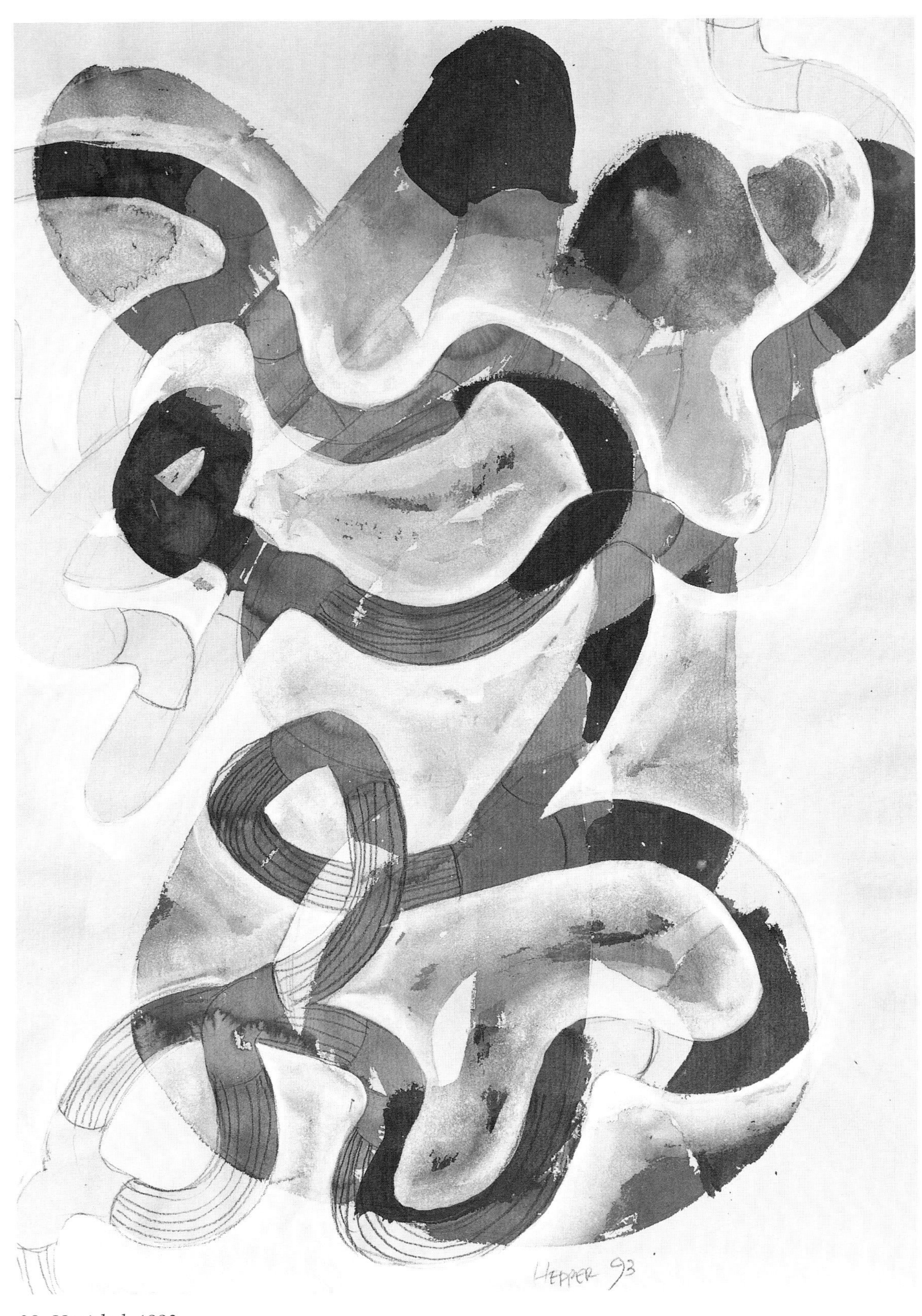

20. *Untitled, 1993*

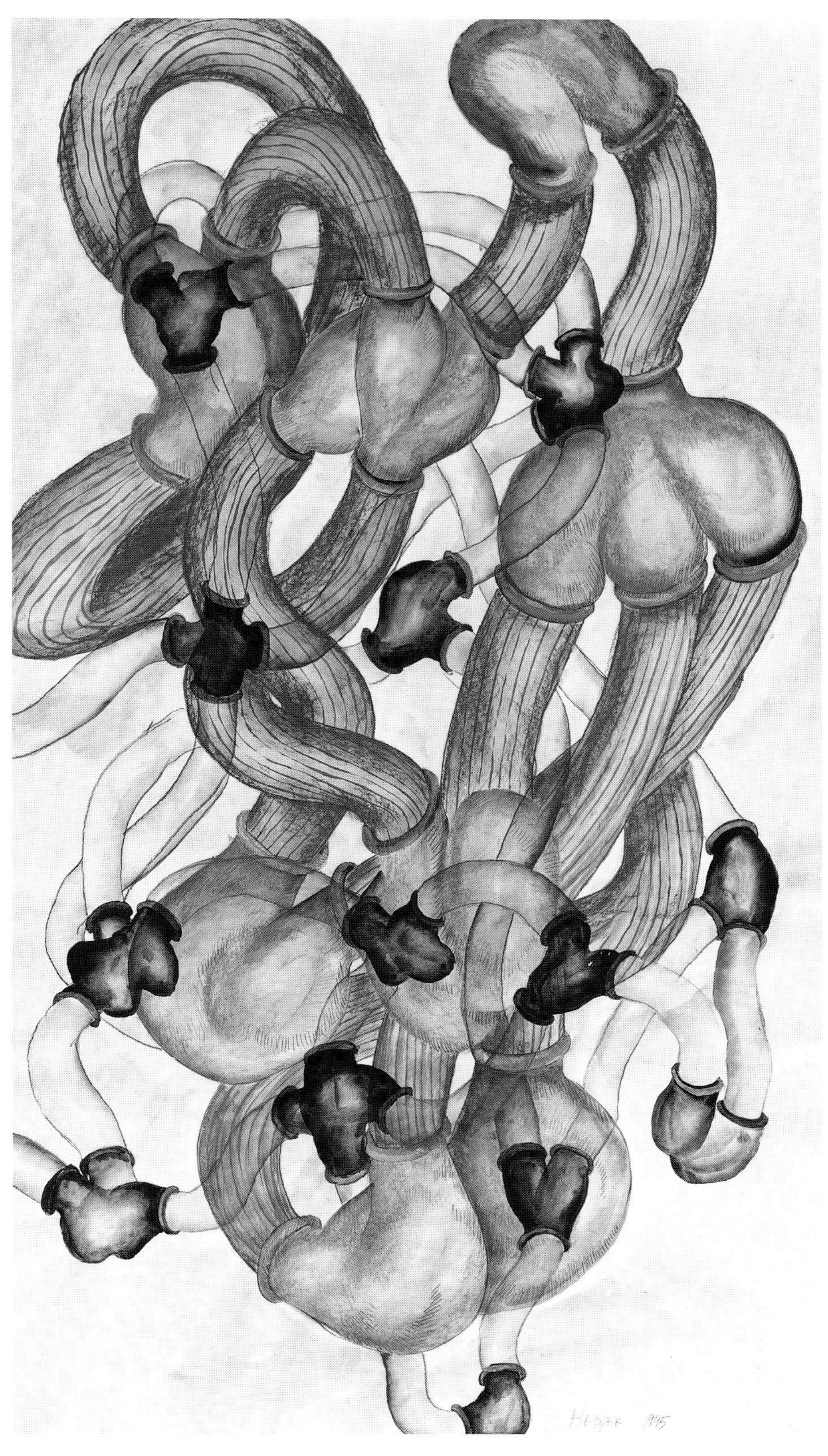

23. *Untitled, 1995*

DAVID HUFFMAN

Born 1963 in Berkeley, California, lives in Los Angeles
Education: 1984-85 Alliance of Independent Colleges of Art, New York Studio School, New York
1981-86 California College of Arts and Crafts, Oakland

Selected Collections:
Private Collections

Selected Exhibitions:
1995 *Broadsides*, Jan Baum Gallery, Los Angeles, California (solo)
Social Engagements:Observations and Personal Narratives, The Municipal Art Gallery, Los Angeles, California
1994 *David Huffman Selected Paintings*, The Renaissance, Santa Monica, California
Lucid, Julie Rico Gallery, Santa Monica, California
1993 Walton Gallery, Los Angeles, California
1985 AICA New York Studio School, New York
1983 Mental Tape, Noel Hall, California College of Arts and Crafts, Oakland

24. *Feels Like Fire*, 1994
acrylic and color pencil on cardboard
36 x 24 inches
Arkansas Arts Center Foundation Purchase, 1996.

25. *Africanus*, 1995
acrylic and color pencil on brilliant white classic paper
35 x 33 inches

26. *Rebel Kiss*, 1995
acrylic and color pencil on classic crest paper
35 x 33 inches

Lent by Jan Baum Gallery, Los Angeles, California.

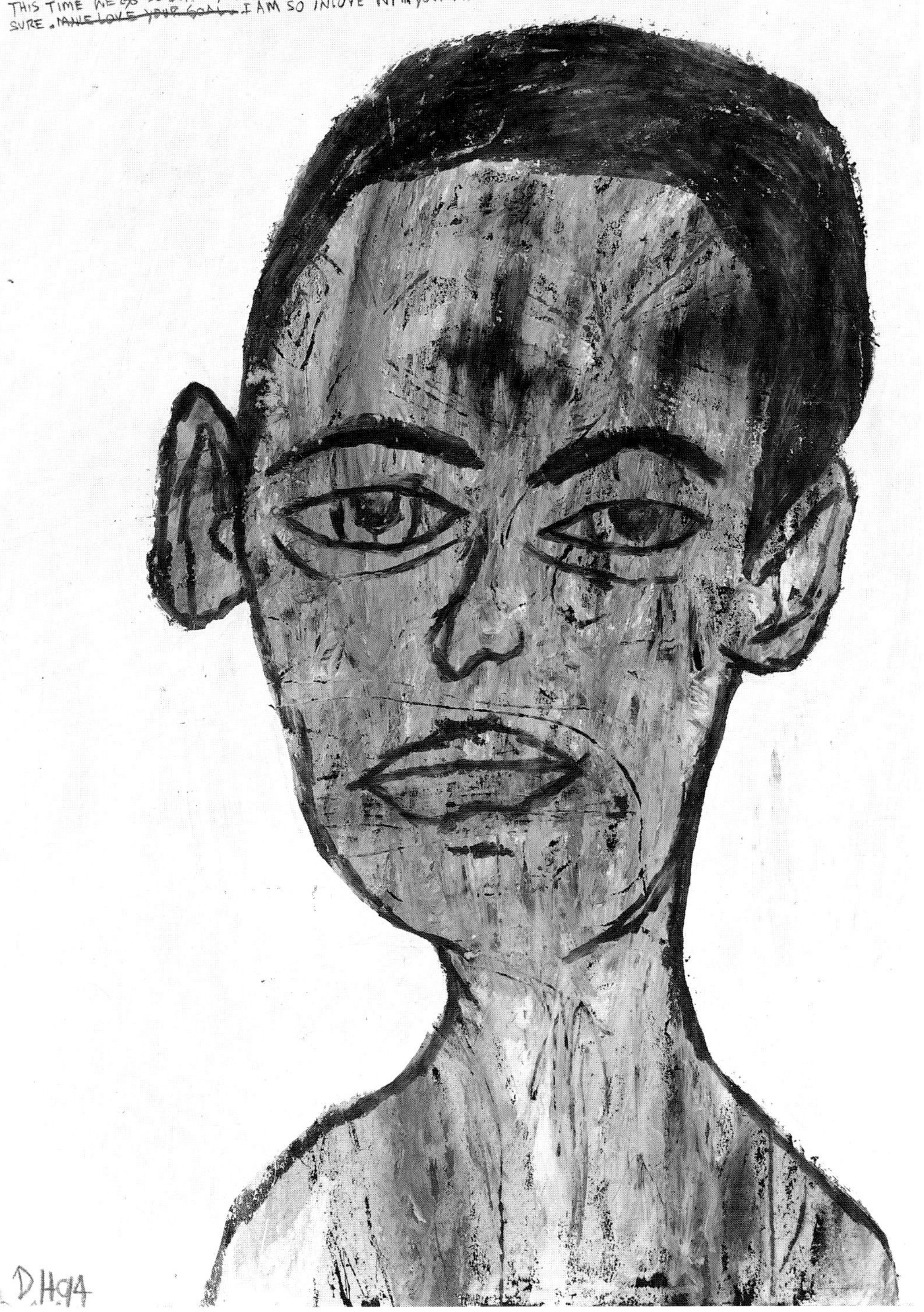

24. *Feels Like Fire*

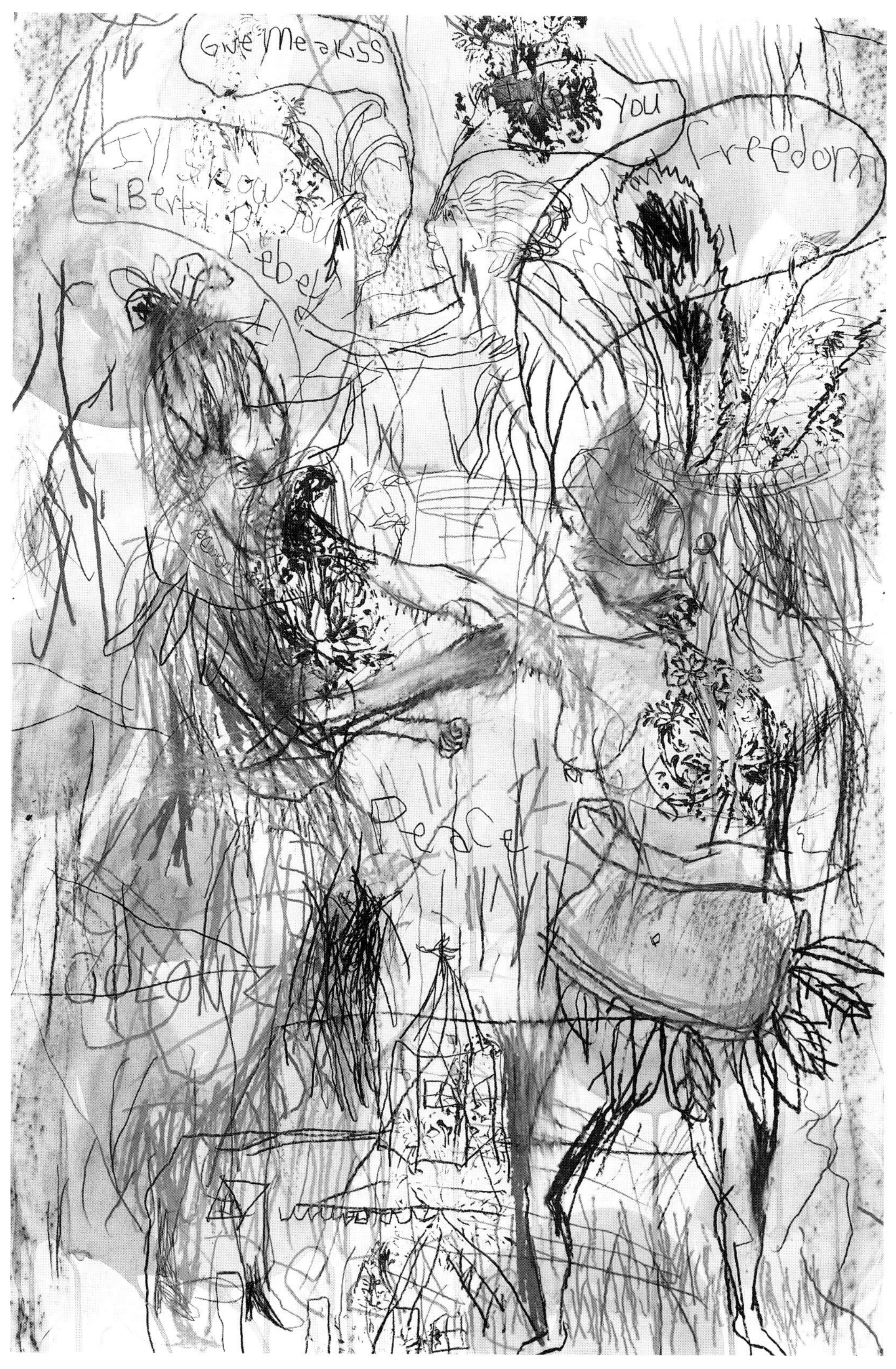

26. *Rebel Kiss*

ELISE KAUFMAN

Born 1961 in Manhasset, New York, lives in Brooklyn
Education: M.F.A., 1992, Queens College, Flushing, New York
B.F.A., 1985, Pratt Institute, Brooklyn, New York

Selected Collections:
Brooklyn Museum, New York
Harvard University Art Museums, William Hayes Fogg Art Museum, Cambridge, Massachusetts

Selected Exhibitions:
1995 *Home is Where...*, The Weatherspoon Art Gallery, University of North Carolina, Greensboro
1994 *Invitational Auction to Benefit P.S. 41*, Loeb Student Center, New York University, New York
National Juried Competition, Provincetown Art Association and Museum, Massachusetts
The Essex Art Center, Lawrence, Massachusetts
1993 *Forced Entry*, Ceres Gallery, New York
New Work, New York, Albright-Knox Art Gallery, Buffalo, New York
1992 Ledisflam Gallery, New York (solo)
1990 The United Arts Club, Dublin, Ireland (solo)

27. *All Fall Down*, 1994
charcoal, gesso, litho crayon, and collage on architectural blueprint
27 x 50 inches
Arkansas Arts Center Foundation Purchase, 1996.

28. *Cabin Fever*, 1994
charcoal, graphite and collage on paper
4 x 10 3/8 inches
Arkansas Arts Center Foundation Purchase, 1996.

29. *Home Series 3*, 1994
charcoal, graphite, and collage on mylar and paper
8 3/4 x 11 inches
Lent by the artist.

30. *House and Home (triptych)*, 1994
graphite and paper collage on mylar and paper
each panel 7 1/4 x 5 1/4 inches
Lent by Lucy and Paul Robinson, Little Rock, Arkansas.

31. *Cabin Fever 2*, 1995
India ink on mylar
38 x 43 1/2 inches
Lent by the artist.

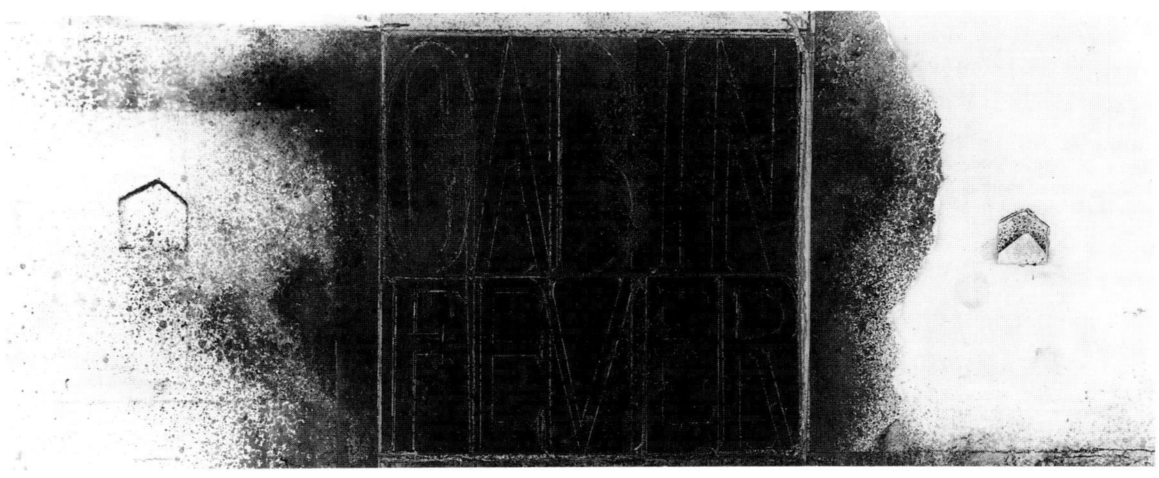

28. *Cabin Fever*

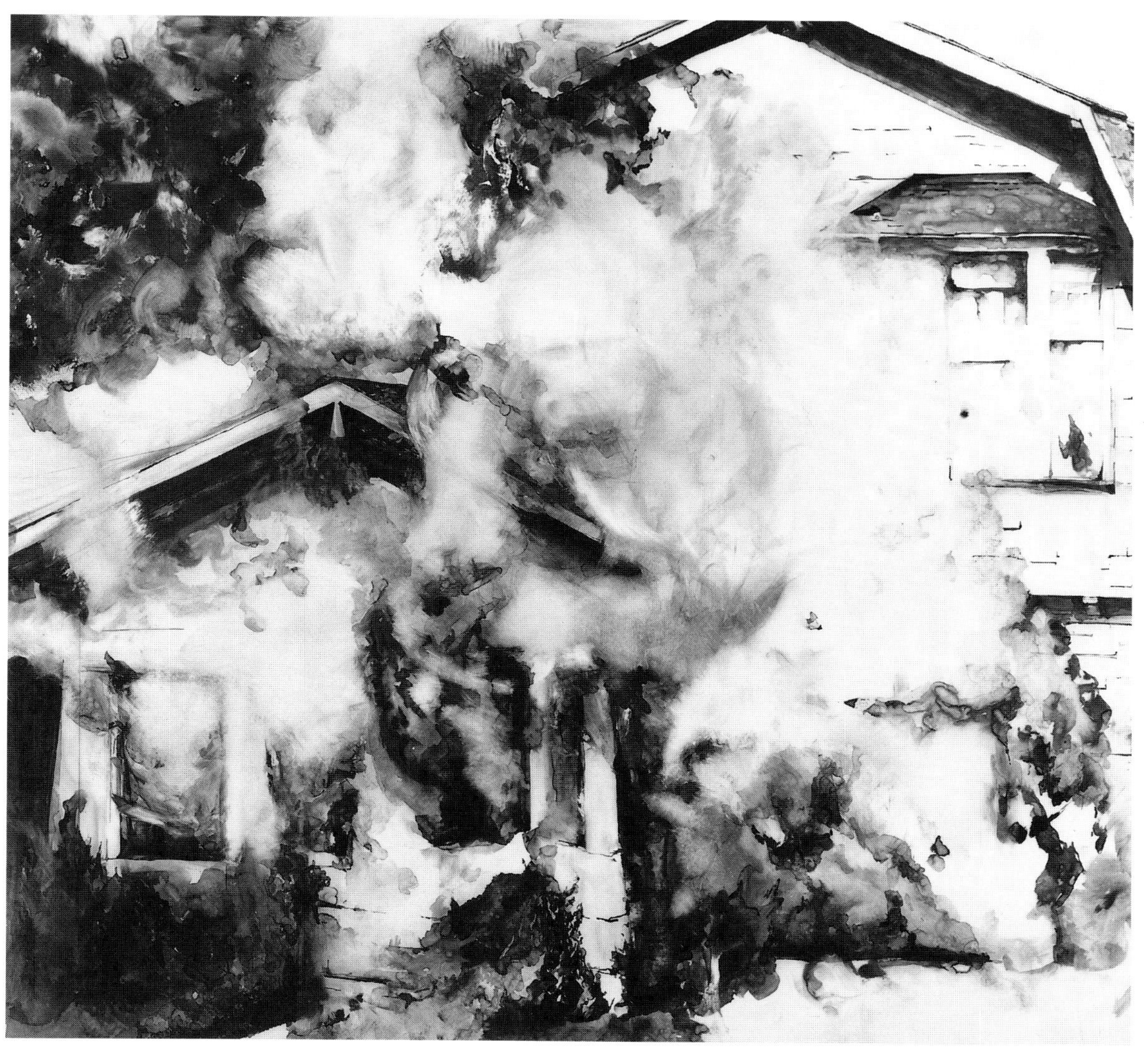

31. *Cabin Fever 2*

IRA KORMAN

Born 1962 in New York, New York, lives in Los Angeles, California
Education: B.F.A., 1984, Rhode Island School of Design, Providence
1985-87, Apprenticeship with painter/sculptor Bernar Venet

Selected Collections:
Sprung, Horn, Kramer, & Woods, Tarrytown, New York
Sugar Museum, Munich, Germany
TMP Marketing, Los Angeles, California
The Arkansas Arts Center Foundation

Selected Exhibitions:
1994 *Recent Drawings*, Koplin Gallery, Santa Monica, California (solo)
1993 Galerie Bartsch & Chariau, Munich, Germany (solo)
1988 Marylou's, New York, New York (solo)
1987 Galerie Thomas Flora, Innsbruck, Austria (solo)

32. *Paul*, 1992
charcoal on paper
35 x 25 1/2 inches

33. *Grandpa's Chair*, 1994
charcoal on paper
40 x 25 inches

Lent by Koplin Gallery, Santa Monica, California.

34. *Sweet Virginia*, 1994
charcoal on paper
47 1/4 x 28 3/4 inches
The Arkansas Arts Center Foundation Collection: The 1994-95 Collectors Group Fund. 94.44

35. *Faith*, 1995
charcoal on paper
27 1/8 x 33 inches
Lent by Diane and Sandy Besser.

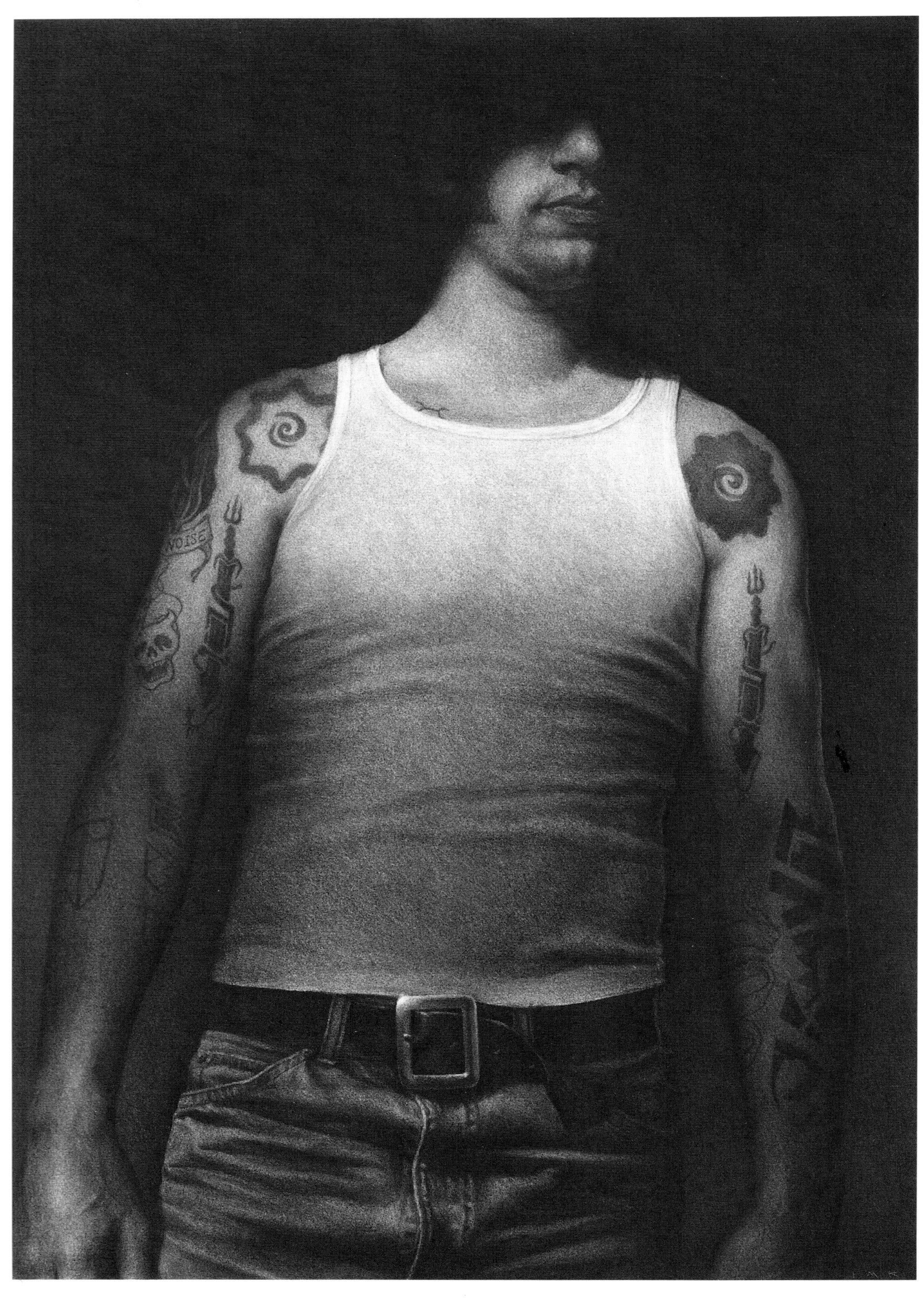

32. *Paul*

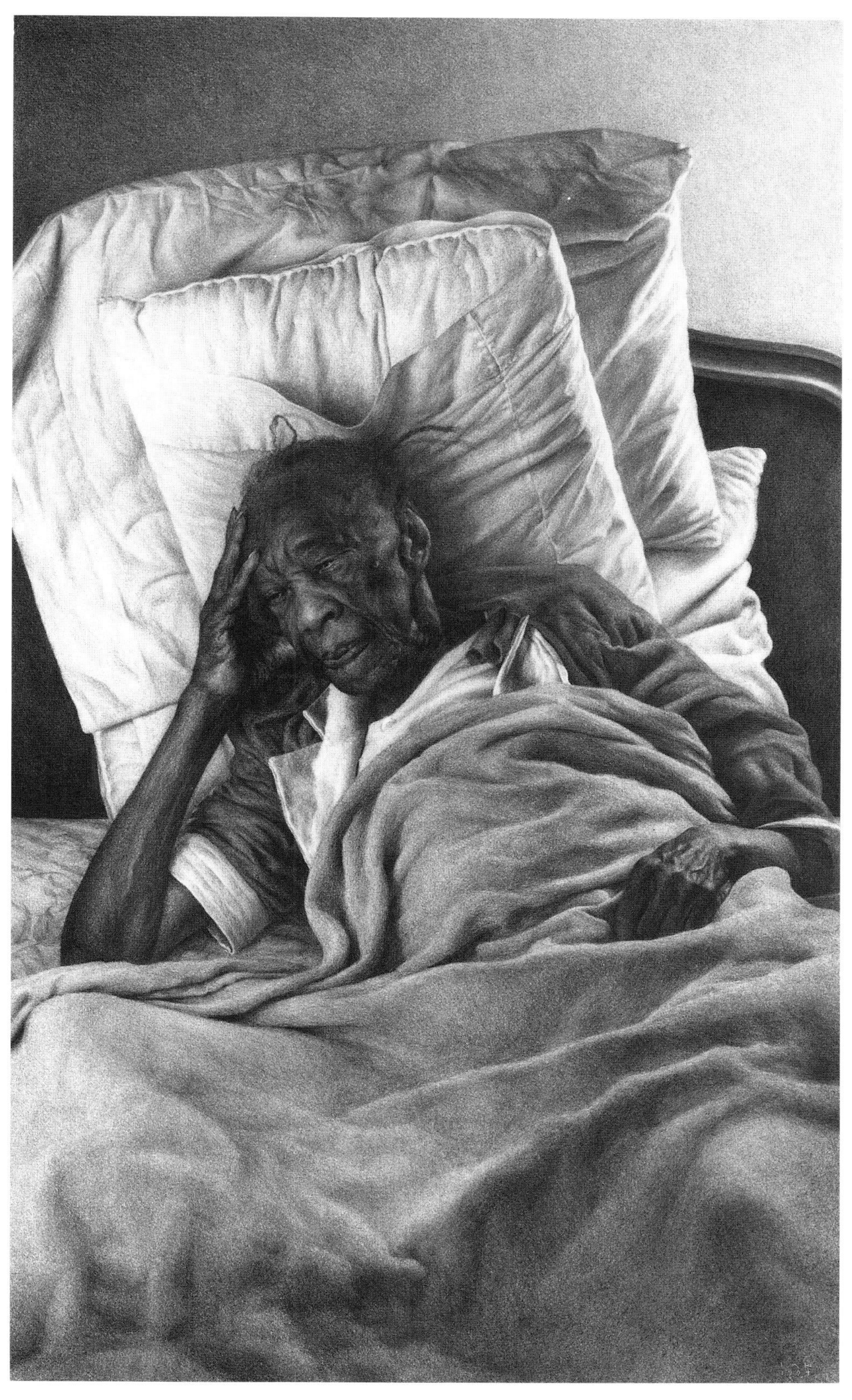

34. *Sweet Virginia*

WHITFIELD LOVELL

Born 1959 in New York, New York, lives in New York
Education: B.F.A., 1981, Cooper Union School of Art, New York

Selected Collections:
The Metropolitan Museum of Art, New York
The New School for Social Research, New York
The Promise of Learnings Collection, New York
The Arkansas Arts Center Foundation

Selected Exhibitions:
1995 *Current Identities*, Museum of Modern Art, Bogota, Colombia
Resisting Categories, City Without Walls, Newark, New Jersey
The Murder Show, Miami Dade College, Wolfson Gallery, Miami, Florida
1994 *Current Identities: Recent Painting in the US*, Cuenca International Bienal of Painting, Cuenca, Ecuador (traveling)
1993 Lehman College Art Gallery, Bronx, New York (solo)
Portraits / Retratos, Intar Latin American Gallery, New York
Duke University Museum of Art, Durham, North Carolina
1992 Allen Memorial Art Museum, Oberlin College, Obrtlin, Ohio
Center for the Fine Arts, Miami, Florida
Madison Art Center, Madison, Wisconsin

36. *Dress With Tree*, 1992
oil stick and charcoal on paper
85 x 51 inches
The Arkansas Arts Center Foundation Collection: Purchased with Gallery Contributions, 1994. 94.20

37. *Snake*, 1993
charcoal and acrylic on paper
67 x 51 inches
Lent by D.C. Moore Gallery, New York, New York.

38. *Hand II*, 1994
oil stick and charcoal
54 x 40 1/4 inches
Lent by Jackye and Curtis Finch, Jr., Little Rock, Arkansas.

39. *Hand XIII*, 1995
oil stick and charcoal on paper
54 x 40 1/2 inches
Lent by D.C. Moore Gallery, New York, New York.

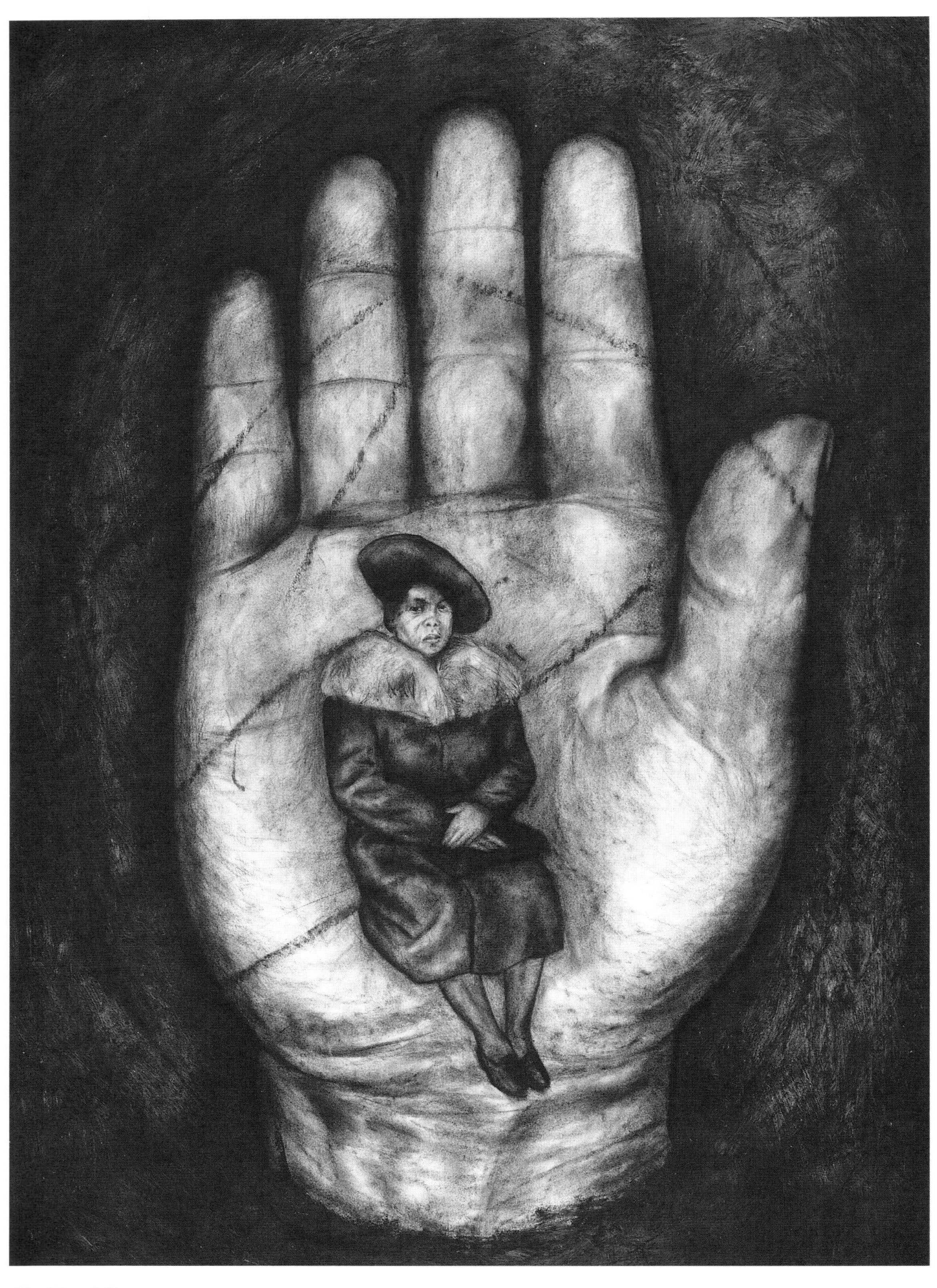

38. *Hand II*

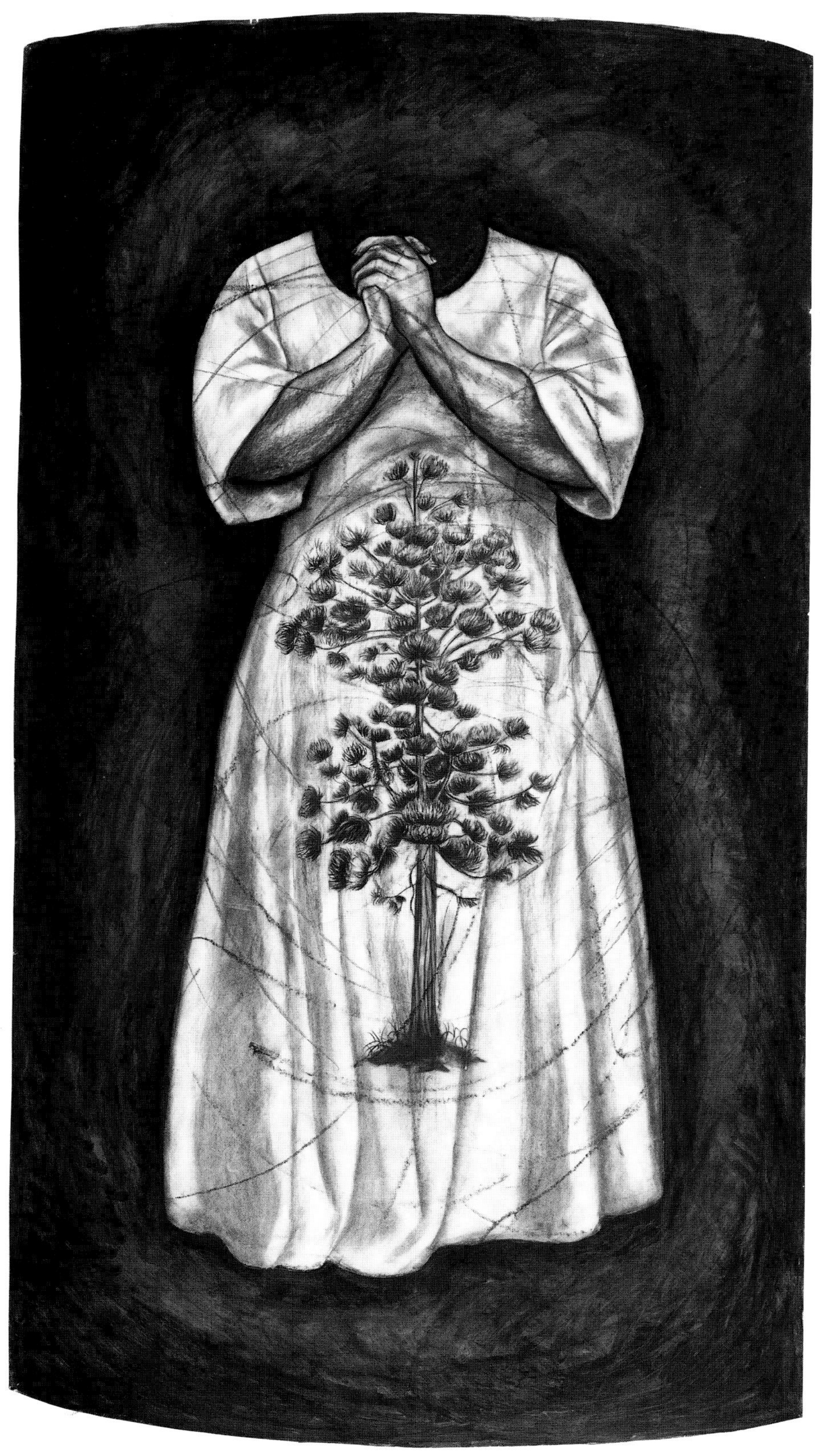

36. *Dress With Tree*

TIM MOSMAN

Born 1954 in Corning, Iowa, lives in Arizona
Education: M.F.A., 1988, Mills College, Oakland, California
M.A., 1985, University of Iowa, Iowa City
B.F.A., 1978, University of Iowa, Iowa City

Selected Collections:
Mills College, Art Gallery, Oakland, California
Saks Fifth Avenue, San Francisco, California
Scheiber Design Group, San Francisco, California

Selected Exhibitions:
1995 Susan Cummins Gallery, Mill Valley, California (solo)
Bay Area Portfolio: About Abstraction, Regional Center for the Arts, Walnut Creek, California
1994 *Drawing the Line*, Susan Cummins Gallery, Mill Valley, California
1993 *Fresh Paint*, Transamerica Pyramid Gallery, San Francisco, California
1992 *COCA 92nd Annual*, Center on Contemporary Art, Seattle, Washington
Visiting Faculty Exhibition, University of Washington School of Art, Seattle
1991 *67th Crocker Kingsley Annual Exhibition*, Crocker Art Museum, Sacramento, California

40. *Loss of Identity*, 1995
acrylic on paper
27 x 19 inches
Arkansas Arts Center
Foundation Purchase, 1996.

41. *Untitled #195030*, 1995
acrylic on paper
30 x 22 1/2 inches

42. *Untitled #195073*, 1995
charcoal, acrylic on paper
44 x 31 inches

Lent by Susan Cummins
Gallery, Mill Valley, California.

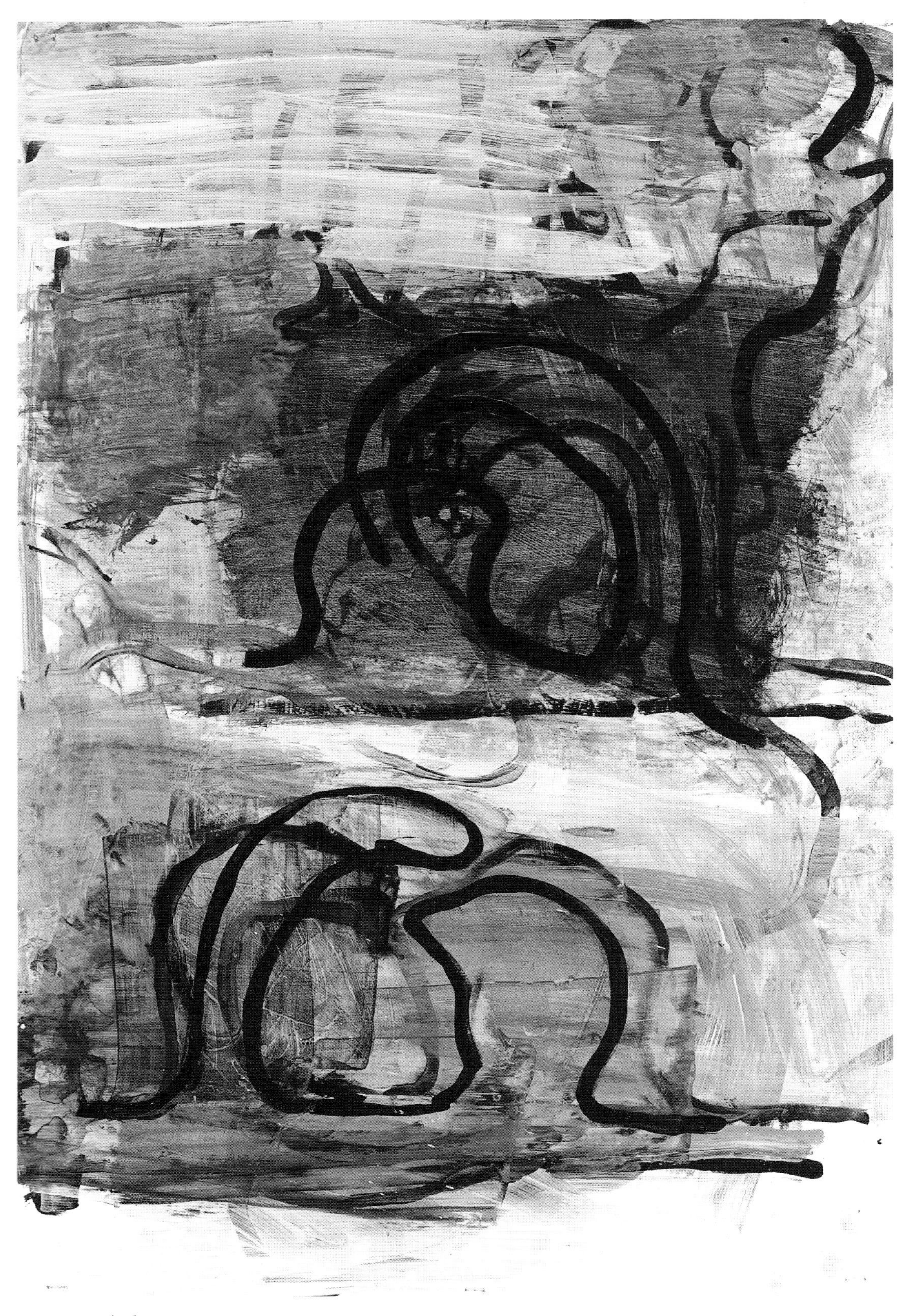

40. *Loss of Identity*

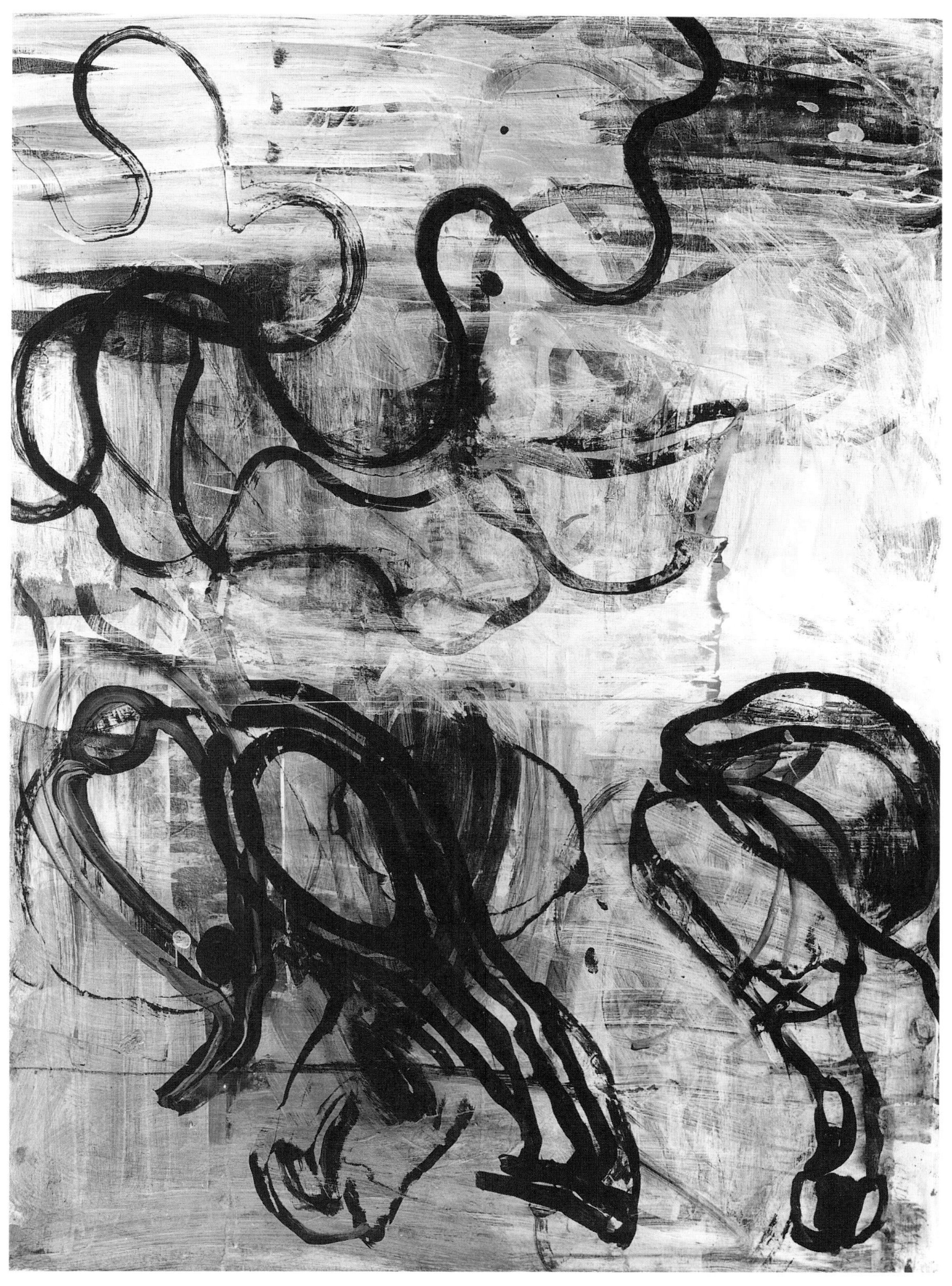

41. *Untitled #195030*

STEPHEN NAMARA

Born 1953 in Kenya, East Africa, lives in San Francisco, California
Education: M.A., 1982, California State University, San Francisco
B.F.A., 1978, University of Missouri, Columbia

Selected Collections:
Ralph Ehrenpreis, Los Angeles, California
Honolulu Advertiser, Hawaii
Stroud and Waller, Inc., Highland Park, Illinois
The Arkansas Arts Center Foundation

Selected Exhibitions:
1995 *American Color: a Late 20th Century Perspective,* Louis Stern Fine Arts, West Hollywood, California
In the Black, Luckman Fine Arts Gallery, California State University, Los Angeles
1994 Koplin Gallery, Santa Monica, California (solo)
Haines Gallery, San Francisco, California (solo)
Lyricism & Light, Palo Alto Cultural Center, California
Drawing the Line, Susan Cummins Gallery, Mill Valley, California
1992 Haines Gallery, San Francisco, California (solo)
Encaustics, Palo Alto Cultural Center, Palo Alto, California
1991 Fairfield Art Center, California (solo)

43. *Female Model,* 1993
charcoal, chalk on paper
40 x 30 inches
Lent by Koplin Gallery, Santa Monica, California.

44. *Adelle,* 1994
dry pigment, conte crayon an paper
53 1/4 x 41 1/4 inches
Arkansas Arts Center Foundation Purchase, 1995.
95.55

45. *Untitled,* 1995
dry pigment on paper
62 x 41 inches
Arkansas Arts Center Foundation Purchase, Collections Group Fund, 1996.

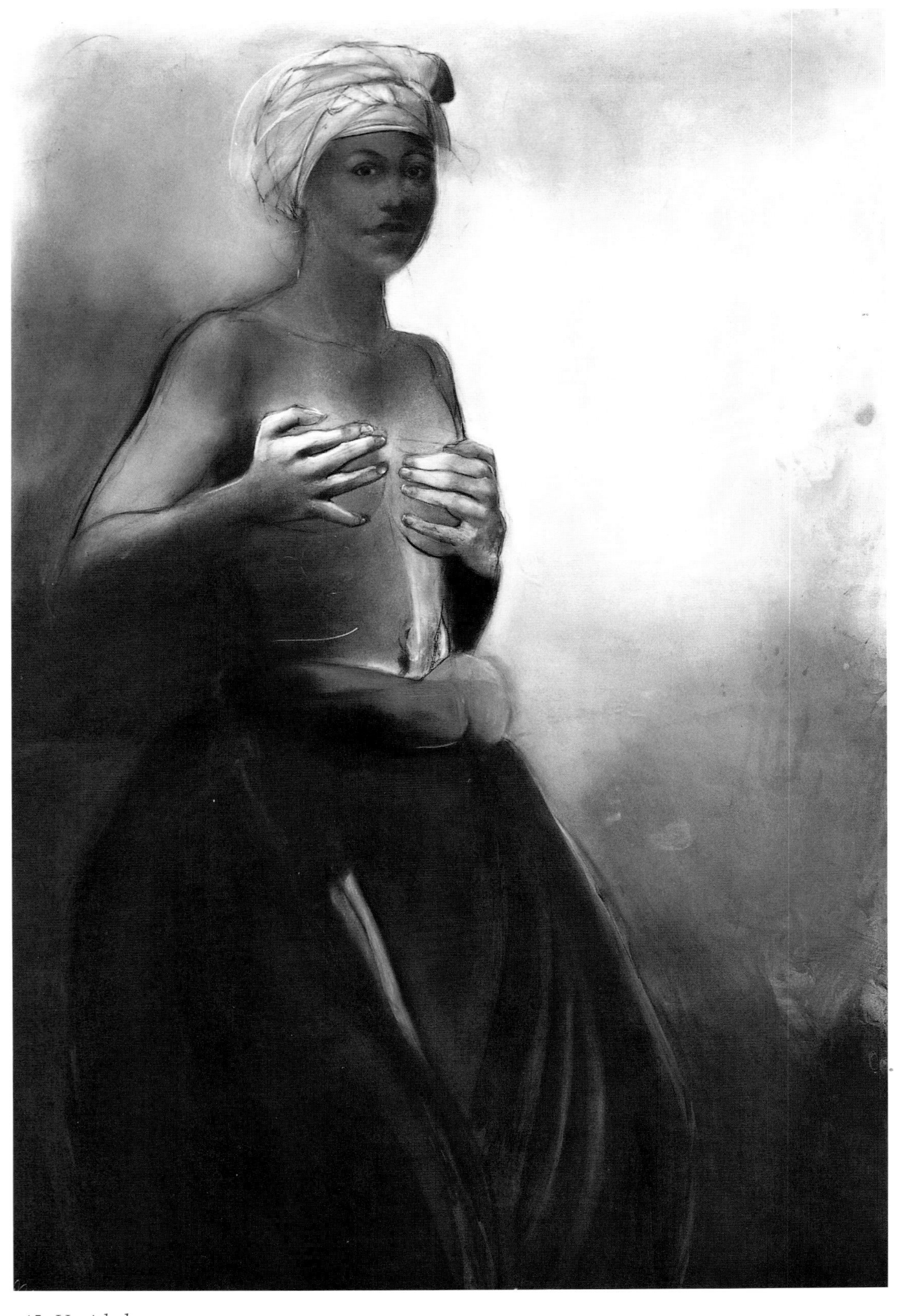

45. *Untitled*

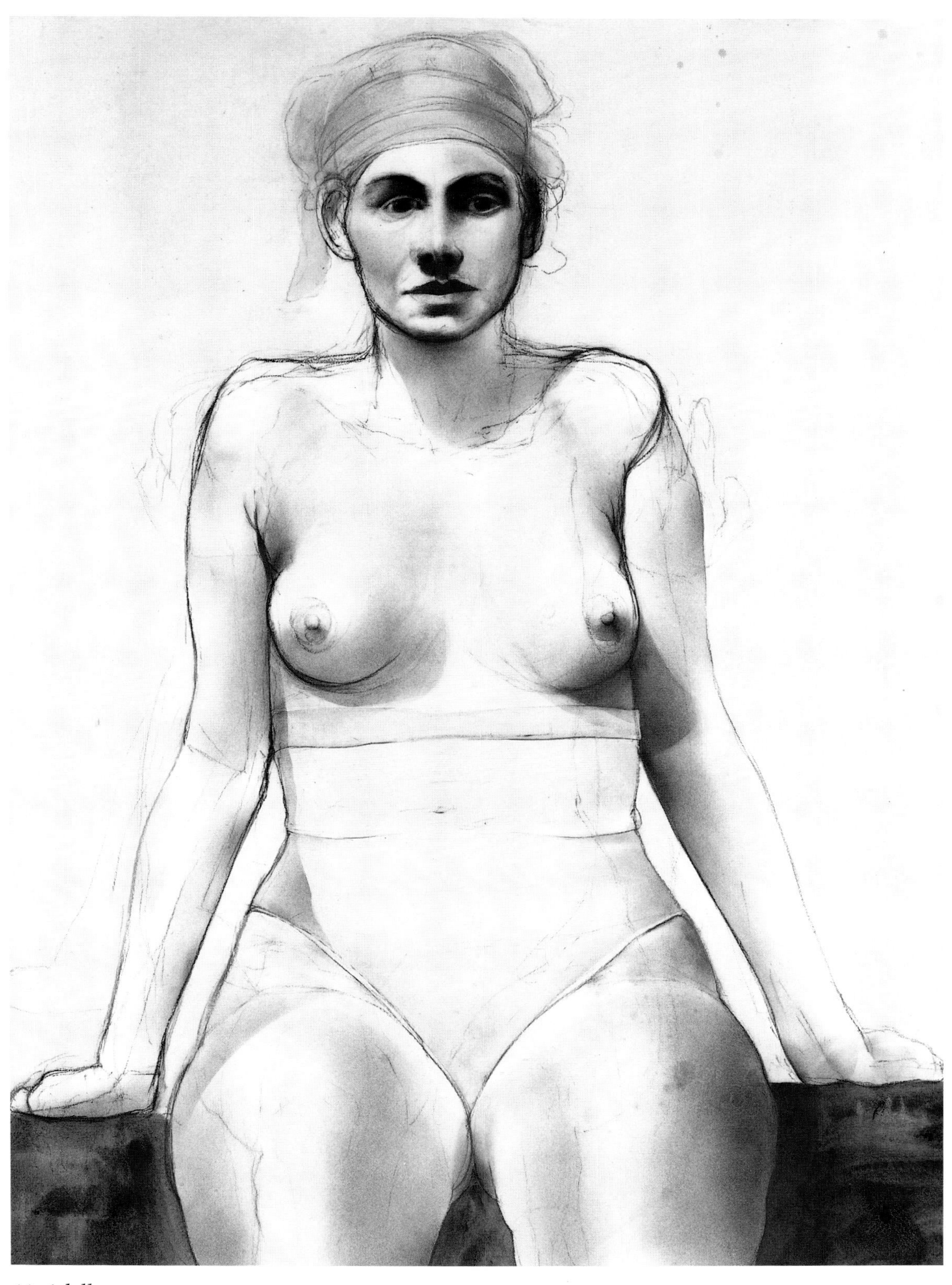

44. *Adelle*

HARVEY QUAYTMAN

Born 1937 in Far Rockaway, New York, lives in New York
Education: B.F.A., 1959, Boston Museum School, Boston, Massachusetts and Tufts University, Medford, Massachusetts

Selected Collections:
Corcoran Gallery of Art, Washington, D.C.
Israel Museum, Jerusalem
Museum of Fine Arts, Boston, Massachusetts
Museum of Modern Art, New York
Tate Gallery, London, England
Whitney Museum of American Art, New York
The Arkansas Arts Center Foundation

Selected Exhibitions:
1995 Nielsen Galery, Boston, Massachusetts (solo)
1994 Haines Gallery, San Francisco, California (solo)
1993 McKee Gallery, New York (solo)
Nielson Gallery, Boston, Massachusetts (solo)
1991 Art Gallery of New South Wales, Australia
1990 Galerie Nordenhake, Malmo, Sweden (solo)
Gilbert Brownstone Gallery, Paris (solo)
Tony Oliver Gallery, Sydney, Australia (solo)
1987 *Corcoran Biennale*, Corcoran Gallery of Art, Washington, D.C.

46. *First Drawing*, 1993
ink and acrylic on paper
mounted on aluminum
11 x 11 inches

47. *Bister*, 1994
ink and acrylic on paper
mounted on aluminum
20 x 20 inches

48. *Wismuth*, 1995
ink and acrylic on paper
mounted on aluminum
12 x 12 inches

The Arkansas Arts Center Foundation Collection: The '94 Tabriz Fund.
95.41.1-3

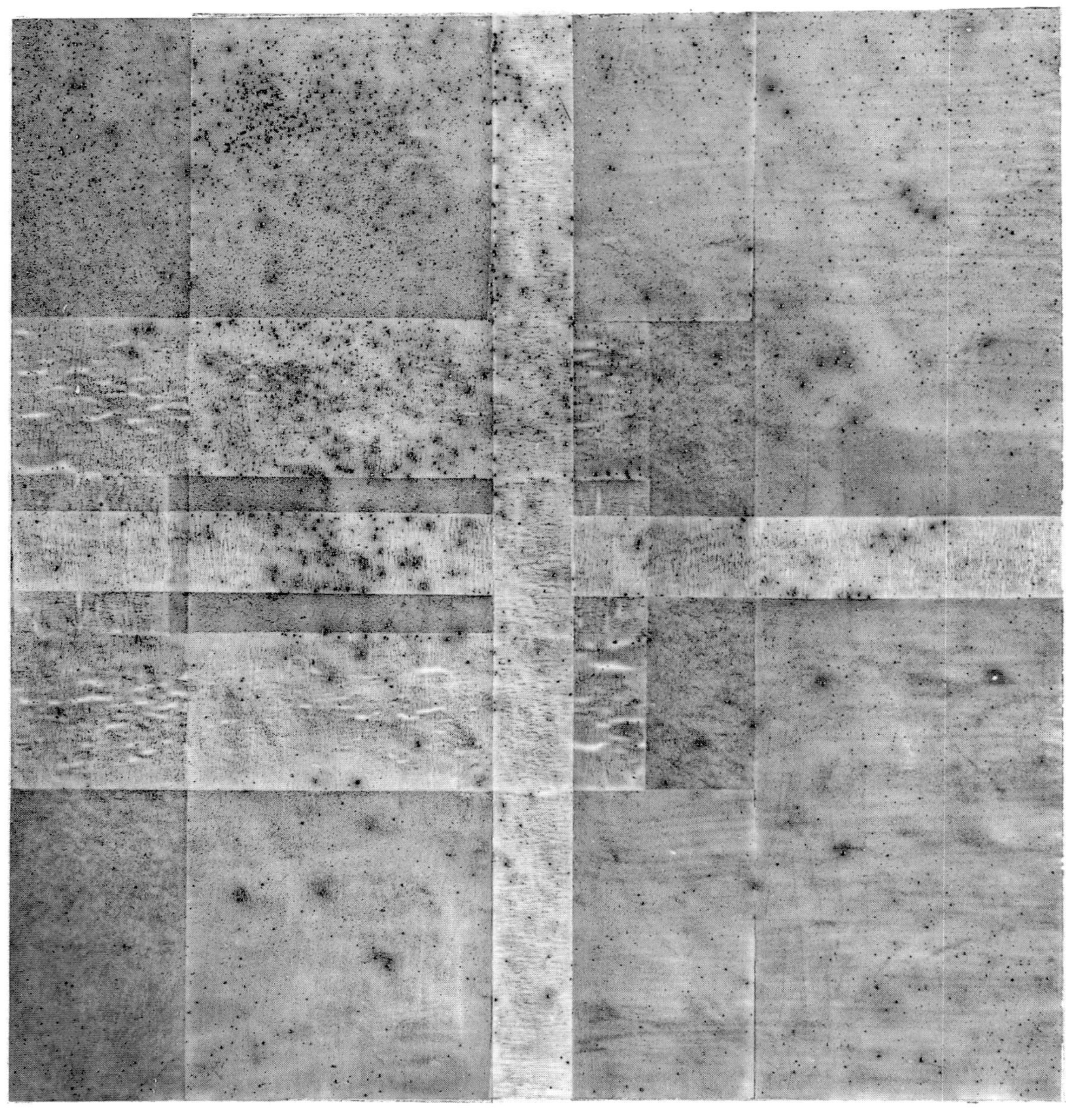

46. *First Drawing*

48. *Wismuth*

THE ARKANSAS ARTS CENTER FOUNDATION BOARD OF DIRECTORS